Dr. Wilson is a popular speaker for sexual communication workshops and lectures on parent-child communication, marriage enrichment, male-female relationships, and divorced living. In addition to her work in sexual communication, she is a consultant and general communication trainer, and is an assistant professor of speech communication at East Tennessee State University.

JANICE WILSON

IMPROVING YOUR
SEXUAL COMMUNICATION

A SPECTRUM BOOK

PRENTICE-HALL INC., Englewood Cliffs, New Jersey 07632

Library of Congress Cataloging in Publication Data

Wilson, Janice.
   Sexpression.

   (A Spectrum book)
   Bibliography: p.
   Includes index.
   1. Communication in sex. 2. Sexual intercourse. 3. Sex instruction. I. Title.
HQ31.W773   306.7   80-12982
ISBN 0-13-807610-3
ISBN 0-13-807602-2 (pbk.)

Editorial/production supervision by Norma Miller Karlin
Cover design by Honi Werner
Manufacturing buyer: Cathie Lenard
Interior design by Dawn L. Stanley
Composition by Jay's Publishers Services, Inc.

© 1980 by Janice Wilson
All rights reserved. No part of this book may be reproduced in any form or by any means without permission in writing from the author.

A SPECTRUM BOOK

10 9 8 7 6 5 4 3 2 1

Printed in the United States of America

Prentice-Hall International, Inc., *London*
Prentice-Hall of Australia Pty. Limited, *Sydney*
Prentice-Hall of Canada, Ltd., *Toronto*
Prentice-Hall of India Private Limited, *New Delhi*
Prentice-Hall of Japan, Inc., *Tokyo*
Prentice-Hall of Southeast Asia Pte. Ltd., *Singapore*
Whitehall Books Limited, *Wellington, New Zealand*

To Zayna

CONTENTS

PART ONE
SEXPRESSIONS:
IMAGES AND ROLES, *1*

chapter 1
Evaluating Your Own Sexpression, 3

chapter 2
Sexual Gamesmanship, 15

chapter 3
The Pseudosexual Revolution, 42

chapter 4
Masculinity and Femininity Revisited, 63

PART TWO
SEXPRESSIONS:
SOCIETY AND YOU, *91*

chapter 5
Your Sexual Heritage, 93

chapter 6
Parental Sexpressions, 110

chapter 7
Peer Sexpressions, 128

chapter 8
Media Sexpressions, 148

chapter 9
Expert Sexpressions, 168

PART THREE
SEXPRESSIONS:
COMMUNICATION AND
SEXUAL DISCOVERY, *189*

chapter 10
The Language of Coitus, 191

chapter 11
Creating Facilitative Sexpressions, 211

Index, 225

part one
Sexpressions:
IMAGES AND ROLES

chapter 1
EVALUATING YOUR OWN SEXPRESSION

The romantic evening was planned. Lights were low. Music played softly. Wine was chilled. The dinner included an aphrodisiac à la oysters and no less than the latest sex book close at hand. Forty-eight attempted positions and three shredded pillows later, he looks at her. She looks at him. He says, "Was it okay for you?" She says, "Sure, was it okay for you?" He smiles and says, "Sure." They turn over to go to sleep. He thinks, "Maybe I can get my $8.95 back for the book. The $22.50 for wine, food, and song is shot." She thinks, "Perhaps a different book."

Naturally you want to maximize your sexual pleasure and provide the fullest pleasure for your partner. That's what it's all about. But what an enigma. Sometimes you get the feeling that the opposite sex should come with instructions attached to the genitals. Well, perhaps you don't feel quite that bewildered. Nevertheless, we all want to be able more fully to understand, explore, and express our sexuality. That is important. Besides, it puts roses in your cheeks, a spring in your step, and a smile on your face—not to mention a warm feeling in your heart and other places. It makes you happy.

Certainly you deserve sexual happiness. But how do you

maximize that to the fullest? It is often a matter of changing one basic aspect of sexuality. What would you guess might make that kind of difference? Would it be polishing up erotic techniques and finesse? No. Maybe becoming physically fit? No. Perhaps getting a sexy hair style for greater physical attractiveness? No. Then it must be learning sixty-eight new and titillating positions? No. How about locating your partner's secret erogenous zones? No. What about communication? Absolutely. Good communication makes all the difference in the world.

Sex is communication. When you participate in sex, you are communicating. Sometimes poorly. Sometimes twelve on a scale of ten. Understanding how you communicate about sexuality is important. It reveals information about your sexual experiences, attitudes, words, and environment. It tells who you are.

This approach to sexuality doesn't rely on the usual whipped-up cookbook style of how-to-do-it recipes. If anything, it is instead a how-not-to-do-it recipe. That is, it advocates that you not continue in habits and avoidances that deny the fullest potential of sexuality. Increase your skills for honest, open, and sharing communication and you increase the ability to relax and to take pleasure and delight in the sex act. Why? Because you have removed the fears and tensions that repress you.

Consider, for example, Barbara and Mark, a young couple who complement each other in their life styles. They converse effectively about money matters, share in decision making, discuss their role needs, and talk about other important matters. Yet when it comes to their sex life, the extent of their talk is mostly limited to the standard, postcoital remark—"How was it?"—which is usually accompanied by the standard reply, "Good."

Both believe that their sexual experiences together are mutually satisfying. Nevertheless, Barbara feels that Mark does a number of things during lovemaking that interfere with her pleasure. She also wishes he were a more provocative lover. Does she share this information with Mark? No.

Mark experiences wildly imaginative and pleasurable fantasies. More times than not, he fails to communicate these fantasies to Barbara. He fears that she would be upset if he asked her to participate in his imaginings. Isn't it strange that these two intelligent people are able to talk about many different aspects of their relationship but that they are not able to discuss such an important meaningful element as the sex act in the same straight, honest, and open manner?

When Barbara and Mark fail to talk about their sex lives, a certain sense of frustration may occur in the relationship. Over a period of time, either one may gradually begin to feel intolerant or alienated by sexual annoyances. Without knowing why, they may drift apart, become irritated for little or no outward reason, take lovers, or find themselves growing disinterested in the relationship.

Because we learn to talk in half-truths, guessing games, avoidances, and stereotypic ideas, open communication is difficult; it feels awkward. It seems threatening.

Of course, every day, inside your head there is a cornucopia of sexual thoughts, fantasies, humor, desires, longings, images, moods, needs, pleasures, and anxieties. By now, you may have learned to accept and even to encourage your own sexual thoughts. But what about your ability to communicate those thoughts to others? Have you learned to talk honestly and openly about sexuality? Oh, you may boast about it, tease about it, gossip about it, make fun of it, or compare experiences. But as a male or a female, are you comfortable with your self-image? Have you solved the problem of how, as a parent, you would talk to your child about sexual matters? Are you able to express your most basic needs to your lover? Is your communication such that your lover is able to express his or her sexual needs to you? If you're like most people, at least three of these questions, in actual practice, feel threatening, uncomfortable, or embarrassing. You can easily see that better communication can mean better sexuality.

Expressing your sexual thoughts more honestly allows greater trust and spontaneity between partners. While developing better communication, use the language you already have, but learn how and what to say much better. You won't create a new vocabulary. Instead, you will establish new language habits. That takes a bit of time and practice. But remember: Practice makes perfect. Don't feel that you're a failure if it doesn't work or feel comfortable the first time. If you don't succeed at first, continue to practice the new ways of expressing. But hang in there. Developing a more positive sexuality depends upon your ability to express needs, wants, and desires to another person. Learning to express sexuality honestly makes a difference. That difference, and how to get there, is what this book is all about.

But let's face it: Communicating about anything on an honest level takes guts. And talking straight about sexual matters is really scary—a great collection of "what ifs." Everybody has certain anxieties about his or her sexuality. We haven't learned to talk very well about those anxieties, however.

Sex talk is laced with myths and, oftentimes, plain ignorance. Why is that? Probably because nobody you've ever known has ever talked straight about sex to you. Your excursions into the realm of sexual communication are likely to be indistinct, undefined, and based upon fantasies and fallacies. And all too often, because you don't clearly understand your own sexuality, everything becomes unncessarily complicated. Look what happens to the simple love story. Boy meets girl. Boy falls in love with girl—but how will boy live happily ever after with girl? And vice versa. You sometimes wonder who can get along with the opposite sex. This sense of frustration often comes from unjustified myths that confuse and complicate relationships and from our lack of communication with each other.

Look, for example, at our sexual backgrounds. We learn to communicate from our heritage and our contemporary environment. Many of these communications, however, are negative about the opposite sex. In fact, you may remember far more negative than positive messages.

For the most part, this sexual information comes from parents, peers, and the media. These sources, as you will see in later chapters, tend to contribute to your feelings of vulnerability. Inwardly, you may be aware of a discomfort or a lack of straightforwardness. But you don't know how to change those feelings.

If you can't talk about sex, you participate in ignorance—not ignorance of sex itself, but ignorance of your needs and your partner's needs. Unfortunately, our sexual information sources do not provide adequate knowledge about sexuality.

Are you well aware that most of us talk very well about sex in the mind but that, by the time it gets to our lips, it may not be the same message? At least it is not the same idea that we want others to receive. It may not be verbalized in such a way that our meaning gets across. Picture this little scene. He says, "Honey, let's go to bed." She thinks he means to sleep. By the time he is out of the shower, with his hour-after-hour antiperspirant readily applied, she is sound asleep. He, on the other hand, is very much awake and considerably angry. On his mental scoreboard, he places a big, black mark by her name. He promises himself, "I'll get her for that!" Unfortunately, he doesn't realize that, because of his vague invitation, she perhaps didn't "get" the same message that was in his head. Or, equally possible, she understood but felt that the double implication permitted her to pretend not to understand.

We sometimes hope that other people will guess what we really mean. For most of us, self-protection rather than clarity is the actual goal of sexual communication. We don't want to be embarrassed or rejected, so we don't make ourselves clear. Then we end up angry at the other person for reasons that he or she can't determine.

The inability to express ourselves forthrightly raises the level of our anxieties. You fear that which you can't express or don't understand. That fear becomes a barrier to your sexual happiness. You then react to something without clear awareness. Our actions seek to protect rather than to understand.

People tend to see human sexuality as a powerful force. Much of the awesome fascination with sexuality relates to the belief that this mysterious force controls us. We listen to songs, stories, and entertainments that say that sex or love has a power greater than ourselves. We fear that if we are not careful, "it" will take possession. We are sometimes afraid that sexual power will overwhelm us. These and other anxieties increase our willingness to avoid honest expressions.

Communication with members of the same sex can also increase your anxieties or displeasures. You may find it easier to talk to people other than your sexual partner concerning anxieties. I remember morning coffee cup sessions with other women. Eventually, bedroom concerns were expressed by most. The conversation revolved around, "I wish he would (wouldn't) do this or that." They easily described the most intimate details to several female friends. Yet they did not tell their husbands what they liked or didn't like. Nor did they care to take responsibility for their own sexual displeasure. Such anxieties or displeasures, when not shared between sexual partners, can turn into significant barriers.

And what about the husbands? Why do you suppose these women didn't talk to their husbands? It is because women are often taught that men don't understand or that the male ego has to be protected. Belief in those ideas disallows the majority of those husbands from doing the one thing that heightens both partners' desire—pleasing the mate.

The lack of sexual communication between males and females isn't even thought of as a problem. Actually, we are discouraged from entering into meaningful dialogues with each other. This occurs when we are taught from childhood onward that more harm than good comes from exposing our true feelings to the opposite sex, particularly our sexual feelings. We substitute sexual gamesmanship for honest communication, and we do it so frequently that we lose recognition of the games we play.

It is sad but true that far more sexual chatter goes on exclusively between males or between females than will ever be exchanged between sexual partners. And the sex talk between members of the same sex contributes to a further lack of communication and builds misunderstandings between males and females. This is because sexual talk between members of the same sex tends to reinforce the idea that males are insensitive and uncaring, whereas females are overly sensitive and smothering. Everything learned by males about females, and by females about males, seems to be fashioned in polarities. In other words, teachings often make it more difficult, rather than easier, to relate to the opposite sex.

We fail to identify the opposite sex as real people: They become, to us, stereotypic images of people. Since we relate to others through those images, sex talk generally builds rather than tears down barriers. Women talking only to women merely propagate the half-truths and myths that women share about men. The same is true of men in groups. It's time to get together—to talk to each other rather than to third parties.

Awareness of your own sexual communicative habits is a first step in learning to improve relationships. To be sure, you may talk intimately with your lover. What you say, however, has been programmed by many years of information about sex, as can be seen in the parent's embarrassment, the peer's bravado, or the media's portrayal of the one-dimensional male or female.

Basically, these sources comprise your learning of sexual information. In many ways, their messages interfere with the things you want to say. You want to be able to talk straight to the people who are most important to you. The communication learned about sexuality, however, often makes it difficult for you to always know how to say the things you really want to say.

Everybody wants to know more about sex. Yet in spite of conversations with friends or books you've read by the experts, you may continue to feel curiously uncertain of what to say or of how to say it. Uncertainty leads to frustration. This uncertainty may not be about the sexual act itself; rather, it may be insecurity about your feelings and sharing those feelings.

I am talking about learning to communicate whatever is best for you in a sexual world. You will receive insights into your own maleness or femaleness while gaining an awareness about the communication of the opposite sex. Whether your role is that of a friend, a parent, or a lover, you will be introduced to information that will increase your capacity for more open talk and experiences: more comfortable, honest, and relaxed sexual communication.

The communication of your sexual expressions is referred to in this book as your "Sexpressions." The term *sexpressions* refers to the total effects of communication on our sexuality: the outward manifestation and expression of your total informational input concerning sexuality. Its effects upon you since the moment of birth have developed into your ways of communicating about sexuality. Therefore, it is vitally important that you understand certain of those effects.

Begin by thinking about these simple statements. Don't respond as you think you should. Be honest. The purpose of examining these ideas is to initiate modification to your ways of presenting your sexual self to the world. These statements will indicate the ways you act and react to your sexuality as well as to those other important people.

1. Males and females can be close friends for extended periods without sexual intercourse. TRUE ____ FALSE ____
2. Being a member of my sex has more advantages than disadvantages. TRUE ____ FALSE ____
3. Members of the opposite sex can't be trusted, and therefore it is necessary to play games with them. TRUE ____ FALSE ____
4. Members of the opposite sex are basically manipulative in their interactions and relationships with members of my sex. TRUE ____ FALSE ____
5. The more I talk about sexual matters, the more I will be likely to engage in promiscuity. TRUE ____ FALSE ____
6. Thinking about sexuality as often as I like will result in permissive sexual behavior. TRUE ____ FALSE ____
7. The more parents talk to their children about sexual matters, the less likely their children are to engage in promiscuous sexual activity. TRUE ____ FALSE ____
8. We are in the midst of a sexual revolution. TRUE ____ FALSE ____
9. A double standard of sexual attitudes and behaviors for males and females still exists. TRUE ____ FALSE ____
10. Society greatly influences the way I think, act, and participate in sexual intercourse. TRUE ____ FALSE ____
11. Physicians, counselors, and social workers are generally competent to advise their clients about sexual matters. TRUE ____ FALSE ____
12. Males are supposed to be more skillful and knowledgeable about the sex act than the female. TRUE ____ FALSE ____
13. The female orgasm depends on the male's ability to bring it forth. TRUE ____ FALSE ____

14. Males and females have similar sexual drives.　　TRUE ____ FALSE ____
15. Males and females are equally responsible for sexually arousing and pleasing the other.　　TRUE ____ FALSE ____
16. Talking to my sexual partner about likes, dislikes, and fantasies will negatively affect our relationship.　　TRUE ____ FALSE ____
17. Couples must talk about their sexual experiences together in order to have a good, strong, and mutually satisfying sexual life together.　　TRUE ____ FALSE ____

The true statements are items 1, 2, 7, 9, 10, 14, 15, 17. All others are false: 3, 4, 5, 6, 8, 11, 12, 13, and 16. To get the most from this book, both you and your partner should individually record the answers. After you have finished reading all the chapters, discuss your responses and share old and newly learned ideas. Use these items as a way to begin discussing your attitudes, feelings, and needs openly.

Pay particular attention to the statements that you answered incorrectly. These may be areas in which you experience anxiousness or uncertainty.

As you read various chapters, you'll find yourself saying, "Yes, I feel just like that," or "I wish I knew how to express that better," or "That is my problem exactly." That personal feeling makes this special for you. Moreover, you will be able to do more than identify yourself as you read. You will also learn to enhance the unique sexuality that is already yours. This book is written with you in mind. From your childhood images and curiosities to your adult pleasures and frustrations, it's a book about you. At times, you will be surprised at the simplicity of answers that were right at your fingertips had you been able to see them. But you will also discover the complexities of your sexual communication. Often they are complex because you worked hard to make them so. When

Evaluating Your Own Sexpression

you can't express needs, sexual problems don't get better. Instead, they build and develop into more and more complicated situations.

The following chapters will enable you to add sensitivity to your sexual communication. Making sexuality a comfortable and pleasurable part of life is a worthwhile effort. Male–female relationships can become better, more trusting. It requires, however, a certain understanding and a willingness to develop honest and meaningful interactions.

So how do we begin? Let's start by looking at the obvious. What is there about human sexuality that has not been said? The truth is that the "saying" has not been adequately understood or expressed. Begin to understand and then to sexpress happily.

chapter 2
SEXUAL GAMESMANSHIP

Everybody plays hurtful sexual games at one time or another. Often we may not mean to be insincere or cruel. We have simply been taught that it is less risky to communicate about sexual matters through indirect words and emotions. Generally, the opposite is true. Talking through veiled images and vague meanings increases the likelihood of being misunderstood. Once the misunderstandings have occurred, you or your partner experience feelings of isolation, anger, resentment, or hostility.

There are naturally hurtful, manipulative sexual games, and there also are playful and positive sexual games. Positive games are easy to interpret: They are for fun, and the playful messages are rarely misunderstood. Hurtful games are more difficult to perceive. They are indirect messages or activities whose real intent is hidden. Let's identify several examples of hurtful gamesmanship. You or your partner are involved in destructive game playing in the following situations:

1. There is constant pressure to behave sexually or coitally in ways that are uncomfortable.

2. Conversations include a fairly regular tone of sexual bragging and negativisms about the opposite sex.
3. Coitus is associated with statements like the following: "If you loved me you would . . ." or "Prove you love me by. . . ."
4. Coitus is permitted "*If* you do something for me" (that is, something not related to coitus).
5. The act of coitus is used to make a statement about the individual.
6. Someone's husband or wife tells a potential lover that his or her partner has rejected them sexually.
7. Someone tells you that you are a better lover than so and so. Why compare?
8. People fear sexual equality. If equality is feared, that individual lives within a "one up" or "one down" interactional pattern with the opposite sex.
9. Coitus is engaged in to get back at someone (the coital partner, parents, society, etc.).
10. People say they don't believe in the double standard of coital behavior for males and females and then proceed to talk about women who have premarital or extramarital coitus as immoral, and about males as "super studs."
11. Sex is described more often as a negative, bad, harmful, or uncontrollable force than as a positive, good, healthy, and responsible experience.
12. Coitus is violent, abrupt, or insensitive to partner's needs.
13. One person's coital needs are considered more important than the other's.
14. Lovers are taken as a "proving ground" to cure anxieties or to assure oneself of masculinity or femininity.
15. Someone boasts about sexual activity to build up the "coital ego."
16. Pregnancy is seen as a proof of manhood or womanhood.
17. Partners feel as though they are "masters," "slaves," "persecutors," or "victims."

18. Sexual or coital attitudes or behaviors are set to "fit" peer norms.
19. Excessive coital knowledge, expertise, or conquests are implied.
20. Coitus is seen as a "persuasion" rather than a mutually sharing experience.
21. Under certain conditions, coitus is all right for one sex but wrong for the other.
22. It is implied that better anatomical features would make the partner a better lover.
23. The purpose for coitus is merely to "use" someone else's body.

Read the statements again. Can you identify any sexpressions as your own or as your partner's? If you see yourself or your partner in these games, realize that these strategies have been developed as a way to mask sexual fears. Wouldn't it be better to learn a more positive and helpful way of interacting? If so, read on.

CURRENT DIFFICULTIES WITH GAMESMANSHIP

Everything about us is changing. The games played as children, the ploys practiced as adults, and all the things we know as habits and experiences are being questioned. Do you, for instance, sometimes doubt that the sexual values taught to you are appropriate? Most of us, when really honest, admit feeling a bit queasy about those sexual roles we are expected to fulfill. Those feelings, however, are difficult to admit because we believe there is a world of sexual liberation going on. Isn't there? If sexual liberation exists we certainly want in on the experience and the freedom. After all, isn't freedom liberating? Why, then, do we still feel a slight uncomfortable twinge inside? The answer is so simple and obvious that its truth and reality remain hidden from us. We feel uncomfortable because we are uncomfortable. Think about that for a moment. Is that so difficult for you to consider?

If you think back, you will realize that you were taught to be uncomfortable with sexuality. Children quickly learn that innocent curiosities about body functions and processes are met by unpleasant reactions. In response to the embarrassment, anxiety, anger, or silence of adults, children soon adopt these same attitudes and mind sets. Because of these experiences, we gradually give up trying to talk or think openly and honestly about our sexual feelings. Instead, we develop sexual messages through games we have observed and have been taught by others. Our sexual thoughts and talk become indirect and confused. We lose sight of real intents and needs. Then, because of our uncertainty, we are angry, frustrated, and even bitter when our real needs are not perceived by others.

Because we cannot easily convey or translate our thoughts and needs to others, we don't communicate in a positive manner. In order to protect ourselves, we develop a complex system of sexual innuendoes, ribald jests, denouncements, bravado, affirmation, or silence. We develop game strategies.

To a large degree, we are not bothered by our game playing because most of the people we know are also interacting on the same basis. We see others communicating through games, and we feel that game playing is okay for us, too. This often causes us to repress and lose track of our own sexuality. Our own personality diminishes until it is only a whisper in the wind.

We don't want to disclose our uncertainties about sexuality. We believe that we are different. We are certain that everyone else has it all together. Therefore, something must be out of tune within us. It seems that others are more knowledgeable and satisfied.

Why do we feel uneasy? Because despite the appearance of sexual assurance, most of us float back and forth between extremes of sexual innocence and promiscuousness. I do not mean that your sexual behavior is either chaste or swinging. Rather, I am suggesting that we are caught in a conflict of emotions, struggling with *images* of innocence and promiscuity. Neither is comfortable to us.

Let me share a personal example. While I was teaching a college-level course in human sexuality, some of the students perceived me as being sexually liberated, whereas others believed me to be sexually traditional. Neither image was or is comfortable to me. Both images impose constraints upon my life style.

Once we begin stereotyping our life styles to others, it becomes more difficult to feel comfortable with our real needs. Whether you have positioned yourself on the conservative or the liberal side, you will struggle, in some sense, with the identification of your sexual and coital personality. You will struggle because there is a movement away from the set patterns in society about sexual attitudes and behaviors—not a sexual liberation but a sexual uncertainty. I am not telling you that this period of disorientation won't move us into sexual liberation. I do not have that answer. However, at this time, we exist in a generation of sexually confused, angry, and searching individuals. And our conflicts and frustrations cause us to communicate through sexual games. It is a powerful double bind that we have created for ourselves. We don't want to play games, but we don't know how to be free. If we give up our games and are not freed, then who are we? We speak and react from inward fears. Most of us are terrified of the phrase, "sexual equality," because we think only in terms of loss, not gains.

The power we now have originates in the games of masculinity and femininity; why interact differently? If we give up sexual games with each other, we risk being seen as we really are. We take down the barriers and present ourselves openly and honestly, without masks, games, or ploys. Threatening? You bet it is!

Then why take the risk, you ask? If you play the traditional games of masculinity and femininity, at least you know what to expect. There has been a certain advantage in that. Currently, however, traditional masculine and feminine communications are frustrating to us because we are in a period of disorganization and disorientation. Although it is a time of crisis, it is also a time of challenge. This period of transition, this fluctuation of sexual awareness, allows us an opportunity to look honestly at ourselves and at our interactions with others. Decide now to give up playing negative games.

WHY GAMES?

It is easier to play hurtful sexual and coital games with others than it is to be honest with ourselves. A certain husband game plays when he tells all his would-be playmates how cold and unfeeling his wife is in the conjugal bed. Although it seems that he hurts his wife, not himself, that is untrue. We falsely assume that his only motivation rests in the ploy to use someone else as a coital partner. The greater significance, however, relates to the inward denial that occurs simultaneously.

There is an unresolved responsibility that he doesn't want to face. Whether this responsibility is real or feared, he won't face a situation squarely. As long as he refuses to deal directly with the matter of responsibility, he can never be free. He can't be honest with himself, with his wife, or with anyone else. He remains bound to a life that may or may not be best for him, but he will never know for sure. Nor will he ever be happy with himself, with his wife, or with any of his playmates. Double bind! He won't face the issue. By not facing the issue, he cannot resolve the issue. By not resolving the issue, he continues to search for that new playmate in order to reinforce that he is not, indeed, responsible for those coital problems. At the same time, because he has some doubts about his responsibilities, guilt makes him stay with his wife—simultaneously, he hates himself and her because he is too weak to leave. Can honesty be ultimately more painful than years of deceptive game playing destined to hurt so many people? Game playing is destructive to both the game player and to others because real needs are denied. Reality gets lost in the shuffle of game strategies.

Game playing can be a means for sexual retaliation. For example, when Susie talked to me, she was, at nineteen, an unwed mother-to-be. She had been in counseling off and on for several years. Her problems centered on difficulties with her parents that had never been resolved. Susie could not live with her parents, and she was unhappy living elsewhere. Her parents were of a very conservative background, and there had been very little positive communication between Susie and her parents. They had never discussed sexual matters with her, except to give vague indications of how disappointed they would be if she got pregnant before marriage. Susie could not effectively handle her hostile feelings toward her parents, but she nevertheless let them know that she was angry. Susie's game playing had a most destructive pattern. She made her parents notice her and understand the power she had to influence their lives. The parents played a game which ignored her sexuality. Susie paid them back in full.

The sexual game player tends to injure himself or herself more than anyone else. The game player attempts to reduce certain sexual anxieties. Frequently, these anxieties are efforts to block giving up sexual power that will make a person less male or female. Don is such an example.

In an academic discussion about the problems of sexual equality his statement was, "Sexual equality would be a world of asexuality." He was actually saying, "I am afraid that if I permit or encourage sexual equality, I will feel less than a man. I need sexual superiority in order to believe in myself. Honest sexual relating and communicating is too much of a risk. I can only be comfortable if I am allowed to call the shots."

Don will always find it necessary to operate in his sexual and coital world by playing little male superiority games. On the job, his women colleagues must be careful not to evoke too powerful an image. He would find it necessary to somehow reduce or annihilate their abilities or personalities. In bed, he must somehow feel that the coital act is centered more on his needs than on hers.

How, you may ask, is this game playing more injurious to Don than to the women with whom he comes in contact? Because his world is based on constant anxieties that women are going to overpower him. He fears that they will reduce his masculinity to an irrevocable level of weakness. Each day he tries to subvert those efforts. He will know only incidental sharing and intimate experiences with women. He cuts off intimate and meaningful sharing in order to gain personal security. The sexual game player always sacrifices open and supportive communication in order to maintain his or her needs for personal security.

Margaret is also afraid of sexual equality. You would not sense her fears by looking at this beautiful woman. You wouldn't guess because Margaret is a most effective and dedicated game player. She has decided to be submissive to men, dependent on men, and taken care of by men. It suits her purposes. But inwardly, she also needs to be seen as a person in her own right.

In our conversations, Margaret began sharing the present boredom she felt about life. Nevertheless, she told me how lucky she was. Her life is the story of a hundred thousand other women. Everything was going according to the American dream. She was married to a successful, busy man on his way up. She gave birth to the acceptable number of children: two. Ideally, a son and then a daughter. She and her husband then shared their good fortune by adopting a child.

Margaret was busy decorating the dream house, busy raising the children, busy in her "Mrs. Clean" role with the house, busy attending all those "fun" parties, busy taking all those "fun" business trips with her busy husband; she even fitted a lover into her already overbusy schedule.

Margaret wanted to take some college courses and, perhaps, to assume a part-time career when the children needed her less. She wasn't sure what she wanted to do. She wasn't entirely sure why she wanted to go, but she took a college class for credit. She loved it. Her husband hated it. "You're too busy for such foolishness," he told her. She dropped out. She took up religion instead—a charismatic movement. She gave up smoking, drinking, and her lover. Eventually, the religious experience was not as intoxicating as was her lover, so she went back to her lover. Outwardly, Margaret was the ideal of the "total woman" wife. But she had a lover.

She was a commodity to her husband and her lover. Her husband needed her charm, grace, and beauty to assist him on his way up. On the other hand, her lover was not successful in the traditional sense. Making love to this woman who was a possession of a successful man gave him a sense of power. By participating in a relationship with the woman-object of an important man, the lover gained a sense of vicarious achievement himself. Sadly, no one, neither Margaret nor her husband, and certainly not her lover, sees her as anything more than an object.

Her pattern of sexual and coital interactions centers in Margaret's image of woman as the inferior sex: a commodity sex. Because she views women, and especially herself, as having less worth than men, she will always be dependent on them to provide her with a sense of self-worth. Her need for the college classes was a very brief, feeble attempt to identify her needs as a person. But Margaret had too long seen herself as an attractive commodity, not as a person. She is dependent on her commodity image as a way to address herself to the world.

Her flirtations are seen as gestures of the gracious and beautiful. No one knows that her elegant behavior goes beyond the coy, playful, cute femininity that her husband and his business associates find so charming. Her husband would be shocked to learn that his completely submissive "total woman" wife had independently taken a lover. Actually, all the signs are there for Margaret's husband to see. But he doesn't want to see. He is too busy playing a game. So is Margaret.

Margaret made a choice. She doesn't want to give up her image as "femininity idealized." People might not approve. Her husband would be upset. She is afraid to think of herself as sexually equal, much less coitally equal, to men. She suppresses her personal needs because men take care of her. If she saw herself as equal, she would then have to become responsible for herself and for her actions. Being "less than" has certain advantages because she does not have to be responsible. Margaret's relationships with men are built on that master–slave premise. The master is ultimately responsible for the slave.

This game provides the males and females who play with an outwardly comfortable way of relating—until the "master" succumbs to some kind of frailty or fall. The game is not suited or intended to deal with failure. Women who play this game are not required to be gracious, accommodating, or kind to men who fail. And this is the tragic flaw in our basic male–female interactional pattern. Male–female interactions must be played out in an almost perfect environment. Anything less is distracting to the idealized image.

Most men are aware that they are also a commodity. If their money-making ability is lost, they become valueless, as does the female who loses her ideal femininity. Game playing is planned for cheering, winning, and success. Remove the outer masks of success and these two individuals do not even recognize each other. They cannot relate to each other. Being together, alone in silence, would destroy them.

It is difficult to sit down and talk about sexuality, usually because you have not identified sexuality as a problem. You don't want to think about problems of maleness or femaleness because you then feel less male or female. That is simply not so. To be honest about your likes and dislikes concerning your male or female role is powerful, not weak. And until you begin to talk straight about your sexual needs and wants, you cannot think straight.

Sally and Bill are an "ideal" couple. No wonder their friends were surprised when the separation was announced. However, that surprise widened into amazement when the ideal couple divorced. Why? If you ask Sally and Bill, they will tell you—and they believe—that they were incompatible. Actually, a great part of the reason for their troubles could have been ironed out if they had talked about those "little" things.

I tell you about Sally and Bill because their troubles are similar to your own concerns and frustrations about sexual communication. Realize that everything you say and do has been filtered through the ongoing process of maleness and femaleness—the way you walk and talk, the pitch of your voice, the tilt of your head, the stride of your walk, your conversational interests. You live in maleness or femaleness each minute of every day. The lack of thought given to this always present influence greatly affects you.

It is your lack of ability to talk about much of that process that makes for problems. In fact, for most of us, and certainly for Sally and Bill, a divorce was easier than talking honestly. Although your everyday sexual experiences will not be the same as Sally and Bill's, exploring their situation will help you to better understand the importance of giving up sexual games.

Sally and Bill met at college and married the year after Bill graduated. They experienced several rough years while he moved up the success ladder. During that time, Sally worked to help out; Bill was tremendously grateful. She was also solely responsible for the housekeeping and for entertaining Bill's business acquaintances. She beautifully fit the description of the perfect wife whom many find so amusing, "a cook in the kitchen, a hostess in the living room, and a whore in the bedroom." The sex life they shared was adequate for them both. They never talked about what pleased or displeased them; they never discussed their fantasies; but they both felt that it was a satisfactory experience.

Bill liked having Sally share in their future. It took some

of the pressure from him. He also felt, however, that it wasn't proper for her to work. So Bill never told Sally about the greater confidence he felt when she worked. Actually, he found it difficult to admit this even to himself. Somehow, it made him feel less a man to recognize those feelings.

Sally liked working; she felt that she was a partner in the marriage—worthwhile and capable. They never talked about these feelings that described their masculine or feminine needs and images. If they had talked, they might have seen that Bill believed that his value as a man related to providing for Sally. Not surprisingly, he saw Sally as an object that must conform to the social value of others. This attitude pressured Bill to continue proving his worth by working harder and harder. Sally, on the other hand, wanted to feel like a partner in the marriage, not like an ornament. They never sat down and talked about their sexual images. If they had, Bill might have recognized that he enjoyed having Sally help, even though he felt that it was not appropriate. Sally could have talked about feeling like an ornament instead of a person. But they never talked. Instead, quarrels over little matters increased—where to vacation, spoiling the children, Bill's demands on Sally, Sally's demands on Bill. Their sexual life, which had never been talked about, became less frequent and less satisfying. Their everyday sexual and coital difficulties were never dealt with and were never identified as the problem. They simply believed that they were incompatible.

Unfortunately, Sally and Bill's story happens all too often. The source of the problem is never realized. If we could sit down and talk with the other person, frequently we would find that our sexual personalities had been in some way injured. Instead, we resort to game playing.

We don't plan to deal honestly with our concerns about maleness or femaleness. Instead, we learn to play sexual games. From childhood on, we are encouraged to play in game activities that adult members have accepted. Children's "play games" set patterns for their later adult sexual roles. Unwittingly, these childhood play activities become the distorted games that bind and limit our personal growth and acceptance. These games become a way of reacting to the world. They reinforce our patterns of adult sexual behavior with negative and hurtful tones.

LITTLE BOY GAMES

Many games that boys are encouraged to play are devoid of tenderness or affection. Games of war, cops and robbers, cowboys and Indians, and even the formalized role of daddy are all played with an expectation and purpose of winning; violence is expected, and killing makes you victorious. These interactions with playmates focus on the win-lose concept, which stresses strength, power, and coolness as primary goals. Even with playmates who are on the same side, one boy must maintain the highest power position, one above all the other males. This male play indicates a struggle to be the best. Play teaches him to achieve through domination, violence, and authority.

Transferred into the adult realm, men continue to relate to other men, and to women as well, on the basis of being "better than." The male camaraderie, although extremely binding, is built on the little boy games of impressing, of dominating, of maintaining an authority position in the group.

LITTLE GIRL GAMES

Little girls are directed toward games that teach nurturing and caring for others and improving the outer appearance. We now have the ultimate in dress-up play: the sexy, curvaceous, beautifully clad Barbie Doll.

Before dating begins, she learns that a feminine pout,

giggle, or cuddle is an effective approach to get what she wants—far more effective than a straight, honest request. She also observes mommy's indirect ploys on daddy: those cute, little game plays. And daddy seems to love it. As she begins to date, she learns appropriate sexual role games quite well. She does not compete, but constrains. She does not speak up, but sits down. She does not play, but cheers on. She does not demand (at least not directly), but demurs. For years, she has been proficient in a most intriguing game: how to be sexy but remain technically a virgin. This rather amazing little game strategy allows her to be "petted" to climax without penetration of the penis. As social images change, this strategy is perhaps less standard than it was twenty years ago.

Certainly, sexual games help formulate our sexual personalities. The little girl and boy games are accepted styles for interacting. Continuing to play may limit your ability to get what you want or need from others. Playing games denies your potential for your own unique sexual personality. Begin to recognize your own expressions of game strategies. You may wish to change your patterns to more constructive interactions.

SEXPRESSING THROUGH GAMES

We play sexual games in order to feel comfortable in our sexual personalities. We have basic games that send messages about our sexual and coital needs. To a large degree, these games are destructive and dishonest. They hinder honest thinking and talking about sexual and coital feelings.

The danger in game playing is that healthy and facilitative communication becomes virtually impossible. The major facet of game playing involves the following premise: "I will not take responsibility for my own decisions and needs about sexuality and coitus." Let's explore several major sexual games.

ADULT GAMES

Quantity of Sexual Talk
Equals Quality Sexual Talk

This is a terrific little game because we feel very much a part of the group and proud of ourselves for being so open and honest in sexual talk. In reality, nothing is further from the truth. The loud, often obnoxious, abstract conversations we share are attempts to hide our sexual anxieties from others and ourselves. The noise we make covers the silent frustrations we mask. The more discussions we have and the more heated our points of view, the less likely it is that we will honestly face our sexual or coital frustrations.

When we talk more about sexual matters, we believe that we are experiencing it better. *More sexual talk does not equal better sexual communication or experience.* Quantity of sexual talk does not equal quality sexual talk or experiences.

This type of sexual discussion is personalized or direct. It deals in platitudes. It never self-describes unless it does so in bravado or rose-colored terms.

The talk involves the coital experiences of ordinary people or celebrities. Discussions often relate the following: "how wild she is," "how pregnant she is," "how boldly she dresses," "how sexy he is," "how sexy he or she thinks he or she is," "who's messing around with whom and why," "who puts out," "who expects her to put out and when," "how good is she?" Newer games include the following: "how good is he?" and "the fine points of how it should be done."

Then, of course, there are the sexual jokes. We use sexual jokes to inform us, to titillate us, and to make ourselves look important in other people's eyes. Not quality information, but quantity information.

This game activity keeps us from dealing honestly with other people. We respond to people as caricatures. We see ourselves in others, and our recognition about their personalities is more directly a statement of reality about our own sexuality. Our identifications with others come full circle, because we then set a pattern that reflects back to the way we see ourselves.

Also, the quantity of our sexual talk becomes an index of our effectiveness in sexual talk. We believe that our "effectiveness" in sexual talk declares the wider range of communicating that includes the coital act. Making this final assumption, then, we make little effort to talk and think straight about our sexual and coital personalities. We mask our discomforts by increasing the quantity of sexual talk in "shoulds" and "oughtas." Our noise is used to cover anxieties, frustrations, and problems. If you do not believe me, sit quietly the next time your peer group is involved in a sexual discussion. Notice what you begin to sense and hear about yourself and others.

The Sexual Revolution Game

The major part of this ploy relies on the "monkey see, monkey do" aspect of the human race. Very simply, this is a game because, whether or not a sexual revolution exists, we believe that there is one. Therefore, we want to participate. We need and want to believe in a sexual revolution. It doesn't matter that we maintain the same attitudes about sexuality, nor that although we firmly say we don't believe in the double standard, we nevertheless continue to live it—and quite comfortably. We may continue to respond in the same manners and with the same habits in order to appropriate masculine and feminine roles, but we still solidly insist that a sexual revolution is present.

Actually, the sexual revolution game is directly attached to the strategies in "Quality Equals Quantity." Our sexual behavior has changed very little. The talk about sexual behavior has completely reversed. The sexual revolution has been a revolution in sexual talk, not in sexual behavior.

Why, you may ask (if you consider that a behavioral

sexual revolution hasn't yet occurred), have we been led down the primrose path to believe and accept this idea? First of all, it is a game that allows us vicarious pleasure. The sexual revolution images fill our heads with limitless fantasies. Unfortunately, we have accepted fantasy as reality and cannot separate the two. Now we must present an image of being cool, regardless of how we actually feel or what we need for ourselves. We must not only fool our peer group and our coital partners, we must also fool ourselves. This takes so much energy that we have diminished and almost annihilated the ability to recognize our own needs.

A Current Sexual and Coital Image, Please

This game can be an extension of the sexual revolution game. The difference is that the former identifies with the sexual revolution and with a belief in it. "A current sexual and coital image, please" takes game play a step further. This game requires looking at the images presented through books, movies, or television and actually living and experiencing those roles.

It is a game because we bypass our own feelings and move to play whatever the momentary image happens to be. For nineteenth-century women, the image was "demure and sexless." Today, it is "wild and sexy." The male's nineteenth-century image was "straight, quick, and silent." Today, it is "confused, complex, and demanding."

People who play this game find themselves participating in the act of coitus according to the momentary trends and fads. They try to include in their repertoire attitudes and skills that are valued by others. Male images often require developing rather complex skills and performance techniques. Female images may involve rethinking one's own experience of vaginal or clitoral orgasm to parallel the latest or most popular philosophy.

Contemporary sexual images are rather unsettled because

traditionally set masculine and feminine roles are being questioned. Males and females are having to make decisions about whether they wish to relate to each other according to the heritage of sexual roles or to brave newer images of liberated male and female.

We now have a choice, and the confusions and anxieties are visible. Presently, putting on images has not calmed or assured us; rather, this has increased our frustrations. We reach for one extreme, noisily defend that position, and attempt to deny our discomfort.

Can you see that by jumping for an extreme we suppress our own feelings and needs? Those images become us. For example, the Playboy Image presents one sexual concept and the Total Woman Image another. They are both designed to tell you how you "should" behave without allowing for how you might want to behave. Both are examples of game playing that builds a false sense of security. It is a sense of security only. These images rarely become so natural that confidence and honest interactions are created or developed.

I'm a Nice Girl

To remain a virgin until the wedding night is the purpose of this game. Unfortunately, females who play to remain "intact" too often, or those who play as a strategy, without "putting out" will experience certain hazards. Constant repetition of the message, "I'm a nice girl," tends to be sorted out as, "Nice girls are sexless girls." Females who play with this message game find themselves having only a limited option: either "good and sexless" or "bad and sexy." This good-bad, sexy-sexless attitude is too frequently scrambled and thus becomes a denial of permission to appreciate or experience coitus. For years, every nightmare and horror story was used to illustrate the disastrous results of not "holding out." All these tales of "a fate worse than death" are described in order to save the priceless damsels for the treasured experience of the wedding night and thereafter. Somehow, those same voices forget to present any information about the pleasures and sensitivities of the coital experience. Once society's permission has been granted, who teaches this willingly virtuous girl to offset those years of seeing herself as good only when she abstains from coitus? Can we wonder, then, about the wife who uses the act of coitus in order to get what she wants from her husband?

I Can't Control Myself

Males find this game very functional. It permits denying responsibility for coital actions. Males employ this approach for coital hari-kari in many situations. Success is related to the message, "My sexual drive is too powerful. I can't help what I do—I'm not responsible."

We have accepted the idea that basic sexual drives are simply beyond the male's control. We believe that the dynamite sexual drive of the male combined with the seductive nature of the female becomes more than any red-blooded male can resist.

He Swept Me Off My Feet

Women can't play the male game of "I can't control myself" because obviously both historically and currently they are supposed to be the ones to control the situation. Therefore, a simple change in semantics twists the game to their court. Change the responsibility from "I can't control *myself* to "*he* swept me off my feet" and, automatically, women are expert game players.

Women really do love to play, because the purpose is to justify premarital and extramarital coitus. Married women can play the game with their husbands but obviously not as successfully as they can play it in extramarital situations, nor can they play as effectively as single women can play.

As for the husband and wife playing, the poor husband has to do all the work! But then many games require an extensive amount of effort on the male's part (no pun intended).

Stud Man

This game's fallacy is premised on the idea that males are *always* expected to be in the mood, ready for action. Their batteries are never supposed to run down.

This game begins on the talk level sometime before adolescence. Players who are the most convincing talkers must keep up (pun intended) the image as the game progresses from rehearsal talk to the actual play. This player may or may not actually be in the mood for coitus with a female, but his stud image is at stake. If he is not constantly in the mood, his macho maleness suffers.

He doesn't get emotionally close to his female partners. Intimate sharing relationships would deny his stud man image. The public image, played for the sake of his friends and his ego, is acted out through his constant conquests with the foxiest looking ladies. Frequency of coitus is important: Sensitivity or affection as a lover is not. He sometimes reinforces his own private, personal stud image by visiting prostitutes who make no demands on his performance, thereby allowing him to maintain his own stud image privately.

The Ostrich Game

Parents and lovers are expert players because the main strategy involves hiding your head and waiting for the problem to disappear. The problem rarely disappears; it merely hides beneath the surface and becomes impossible to deal with. Parents play this game with their children for years—from the first sexual question until the child leaves home. Lovers play, too, and for prolonged periods of time. They never get around to discussing any problematic part of their coital lives together. Perhaps it will go away. It never does.

The player who participates really asks for trouble and usually gets exactly that! Parents find their children involved in sexual and coital distortions and misconducts, sometimes in situations that affect their total life experiences. Lovers who choose to play the Ostrich Game often discover that they let the problem slide until the relationship itself is dissolved.

SYMPTOMS OF GAME PLAYING

We are all guilty of game playing to one degree or another. Game playing occurs when we feel threatened. For certain people, however, sexual game playing is not merely an occasional protective device. Rather, it is a standard way of operating. When you interact in game strategies, you experience the sexual and coital personality in two basic patterns:

1. *My thinking, talking, and messages to members of the opposite sex are frequently "one-down" or "put-down" communication to that person.* Females, when talking to males, mentally or verbally discard that male's ideas as chauvinistic, patronizing, or egotistic. Males, when talking to females, discount their conversations as silly, bitchy, or overly emotional. Any time you are placing another person in a "less than" or "one-down" position, the mood is set for game playing. In fact, honesty and mutual communication is completely cut off.
2. *My thinking, talking, or messages to members of the opposite sex are frequently on the basis of placing them in a "one-up" position and of seeing myself as "less than."* In conversations with members of the opposite sex, you evaluate your ideas, thoughts, and interests as being less meaningful or important in comparison to

the other person's ideas. You do not see communication as an exchange of ideas. Rather, you see it as a comparative event where you always come out the loser.

Concentrate on your interactions with members of the opposite sex for a week. Keep a daily journal of your conversations with the opposite sex. Record situations when you experience a "one-up" or "one-down" position. Write out important aspects of those conversations. Also, note the emotions you feel in these conversations. Decide, then, at the end of the week whether you are a serious sexual game player. If so, do you want to change?

CHANGING YOUR SEXUAL AND COITAL GAME PLAYING

We all play destructive and dishonest sexual games. Game playing, however, doesn't have to be a defensive part of your interacting with others. You can gain effectiveness and comfort in sexual communication. Those confused, angry barriers between yourself and members of the opposite sex can be overcome. How do you react and relate to others? Think about the kinds of communications you have with the opposite sex. What do you do that doesn't get you the appreciation, respect, emotional regard, or feelings of personal comfort you want? Here are five steps that will help you to recognize and change communication barriers between yourself and others.

1. *Awareness of body reactions.* Become aware of your body responses and reactions to others. Your body picks up and reacts to cues and signs that you try to ignore. Begin noting signs of discomfort: a knot in your stomach, tenseness in your shoulders, tightness in your chest, and so on.

2. *Awareness of the interactional event.* Once you are aware of your body feelings, then notice what you are physically reacting to. Begin to examine and explore what is going on when these body feelings happen.
3. *Create mental images.* Try to imagine yourself and the person or persons with whom you are interacting in terms of being "smaller than" or "larger than." Do you visualize yourself as being smaller than or larger than others during these communications? If you have an image of yourself being "smaller than," you are interacting in an inferior, one-down position. You will probably be responded to in that manner. Conversely, if you have an image of yourself being "larger than," you are interacting in a superior, one-up position. Either way, you are not participating in mutual communication.
4. *Resolution.* Try to move that image to an "equal space" — neither "smaller than" nor "larger than." Begin to experience how much more comfortable that is for you. Resolve to keep yourself in an equal position. Don't move back to either of the extremes.
5. *Communicative action.* You will not always be able to move to a more effective manner of communicating while the actual conversation is going on. Sometimes we are too caught up in the communicative event to change ineffective patterns during tense interactions. Don't be discouraged. You didn't learn to communicate through sexual games overnight—and you will not instantly change overnight. If you are not at first able to complete these five steps during interactions with the opposite sex, try what I call the second line of attack. When you did not communicate as you had wished, go through the conversation in the privacy of your home. See the situation occurring exactly as you want. Then, if it is necessary, go back to that person and indicate that you were not clear about your feelings or intentions. Then say what you want to say. If you attempt to talk honestly several times, it

will become a natural and comfortable part of your interactional patterns.

Our sexual and coital personalities are the parts of us that require intimacy, sharing, and closeness with others. Those qualities set us apart from all other creatures because we plan our lives in such a way that we give and receive from others. We relate through maleness or femaleness in such a way that others will want to share our life experiences with us. Our sexuality is us, and we become the definition we give to that sexuality. The strength, empathy, sensitivity, harmony, and rejoicing that are expressed and given between males and females deserve exploration, awareness, and understanding.

Decide for yourself that it is worth it! It is. You don't have to play sexual games. You can learn to be honest, comfortable, and equal in your sexpressions.

SELECTED REFERENCES

Abernathy, Virginia. "Feminists' Heterosexual Relationships: More on Dominance." *Archives of General Psychiatry* 35 (April 1978): 435–438.

Andreas, Carol. *Sex and Caste in America.* Englewood Cliffs, N.J.: Prentice-Hall, 1971.

Balswick, Jack O., and **Peek, Charles W.** "The Inexpressive Male: A Tragedy of American Society." *Family Coordinator* 20 (October 1971): 363–368.

Bednarik, Karl. *The Male in Crisis.* Translated by Helen Sebba. New York: Knopf, 1970.

Berne, Eric. *Sex in Human Loving.* New York: Pocket Books, 1970.

Clifford, Ruth E. "Sex as a Chore." *Medical Aspects of Human Sexuality* 13 (May 1977): 57–61.

Delora, Joann S., and Delora, Jack R., eds. *Intimate Life Styles: Marriage and its Alternatives.* Santa Monica, Calif.: Goodyear, 1972.

Everett, Haney Coffin. "Competition in Bed." *Medical Aspects of Human Sexuality* 5 (April 1971): 10–22.

Fasteau, Marc Feigen. *The Male Machine.* New York: McGraw-Hill, 1974.

Fiasche, Angel. "Sex in the Slums." *Medical Aspects of Human Sexuality* 7 (September 1973): 88–97.

Gross, Alan E. "The Male Role and Heterosexual Behavior." *Journal of Social Issues* 34 (1978): 87–107.

Kanin, Eugene J.; Davidson, Karen R.; and Scheck, Sonia R. "A Research Note on Male–Female Differentials in the Experience of Heterosexual Love." *Journal of Sex Research* 6 (February 1970): 64–72.

Kennedy, Eugene C. *The New Sexuality: Myths, Fables, and Hang-ups.* Garden City, N.Y.: Doubleday, 1972.

Oakley, Ann. *Sex, Gender, and Society.* New York: Harper & Row, Pub., 1972.

Olsen, Edward H. et al. "How Do Men Contribute to Their Wives' Frigidity?" *Medical Aspects of Human Sexuality* 8 (March 1974): 82–104.

Peplau, Letitia Anne; Rubin, Zack; and Hill, Charles T. "Sexual Intimacy in Dating Relationships." *Journal of Social Issues* 33 (1977): 86–109.

Rosenbaum, Salo. "Pretended Orgasm." *Medical Aspects of Human Sexuality* 4 (April 1970): 84–96.

Rudy, Arthur J., and **Peller, Robert.** "Men's Liberation." *Medical Aspects of Human Sexuality* 6 (September 1972): 84–93.

Scales, Peter. "Males and Morals: Teenage Contraception Behavior Amid the Double Standard." *Family Coordinator* 26 (July 1972): 211–222.

chapter 3
THE PSEUDOSEXUAL REVOLUTION

Here's a riddle for you: What's old, new, and not yet begun? Give up? Then read on, because you are probably living the answer: the pseudosexual revolution.

The sexual revolution has occurred, and, at the same time, it hasn't occurred. Does this sound confusing? Well, so is the current reality. You believe in a sexual revolution that relates only to "doing it more" and doing it more openly. More of the same thing makes for interesting conversation, but it scarcely heralds the arrival of a revolution.

There has been, however, a pseudosexual revolution that might be described in terms of "more or less" sexual activity; but people have remained grounded in age-old double standard patterns. The fact that more people now admit premarital and extramarital coitus hasn't changed their personal interactions. The fact that more people openly live together hasn't changed society's attitude that it is less desirable than marriage. The fact that more people are talking about their sexual lives hasn't changed the basic language that defines male and female sexuality. In other words, behaviors remain basically the same. We are simply talking more about those behaviors.

Who tells you that there has been a revolution? The media, that's who. They talk to you constantly about the sexual revolution. But do you ask, "Where is that revolution?" Think about it for a moment. Shouldn't you be able to see a radical turnaround, a reversal of life styles? Where is that turnaround? That reversal? A revolution may be on the horizon, but we lack new or revolutionary ways for males and females to communicate—that is, we lack a change from double standard interactions.

You talk about a revolution that does not exist. You pay verbal homage to it, but where is its reality? Believing in a pseudosexual revolution while interacting through double standard values can bring about serious problems. Consider, for example, Alice, who fancied the sexual revolution presented by the increasing numbers of couples who live together with no strings attached. In accepting this definition and attempting to experience it, she denied her own feelings. As a graduate student, she lived at different times with two male friends. She wasn't comfortable in the arrangements. Her belief in the revolution, however, left her with no way to object.

In Alice's case, trying to step into her self-defined revolution was a mistake. For her, the revolution was an illusion—a vicarious experience. "Giving herself" in coitus was the hidden step to a future commitment. As initial hints about a legal commitment failed, she resorted to storms of tears about her partner's lack of love and concern. Both relationships ended badly in unresolved, bitter feelings of anger.

Alice's pseudosexual revolution hid unfair hopes for marriage. By pretending to hold the philosophy of "no strings attached," she created a strong bondage for herself and her partners that could not be openly dealt with. Invisible strings did not permit necessary personal growth and freedom. Espousing a sexual revolution doctrine denied honesty of expression, even for herself. Interactions were limited to ploys, games, half-truths, and lies. She believed, in principle, in the pseudosexual revolution. But, unfortunately, she didn't live it.

Don't be caught in the limitations of a pseudosexual

revolution or in double standard thinking. Desire, instead, a revolution that creates personal liberation. More or less doesn't constitute liberation. In fact, thinking along these lines inhibits personal freedom.

Double standard differences make us unequal in caring and status. Different is not synonymous with unequal. The double standard inequalities have too long been a barrier to sharing relationships. Please understand, I do not negate the sensuous mysteries or the natural differences that create partners' appreciation and enjoyment of each other. Rather, I encourage you to develop sensitivity without the inequalities of the double standard.

Communication is a circular process. What affects one person also affects the other. Double standard communication inhibits beautiful spontaneity and trust between partners.

THE MEDIA REVOLUTION

The revolution has been a paper and celluloid revolution—a media revolution. Show and tell has been the emphasis because the media discovered what we want to know. Our curiosities, insecurities, and desires to solve sexual problems made us ready for the media's affirmation that a sexual revolution was taking place. We willingly took the mysteries of the bedroom into the parlor for games. And we felt grownup in doing so. We felt a sigh of relief, knowing that our old hangups and sexual problems were finally coming to an end. After centuries of struggle, we believed we had come of age. Unfortunately, someone neglected to tell us that the revolution we talked about was talk—nothing else.

While the media was playing sexual peek-a-boo with us as the twentieth century progressed, two publications in 1953 made way for the sexual whirlwind that became known as the Revolution. Can you guess the names of those publications? If you named *Playboy* magazine and Alfred Kinsey's *Sexual*

Behavior of the Human Female, give yourself a star, because you are absolutely correct.

Kinsey's work stripped away the self-conscious mystique of wondering how we compared with others. How could we be confident when we couldn't compare? How did we rate: inferior, average, or superior? What was good; what was bad? What was right; what was wrong? We had little way of knowing except by way of insincere, bravado conversations. Basically, we knew that everybody willingly lied in order to add a little sparkle and spice to the subject. So we participated in those conversations and went away feeling unenlightened.

Then along came Kinsey's work. Whatever we wanted to know—frequency, positions, number of partners—everything about how we compared was right there in print. And the book wasn't titillating fiction. It was about people's real life sexual patterns, all laid out in statistics. Sexual averages became part of the public domain. These averages were the conversation from coast to coast—at home, in the office, from the pulpit. Americans were free at last to cast aside the last remnants of social interaction taboos about sexuality. We wanted and needed to be convinced that what we were doing, or what we wanted to do, was being done by others.

Kinsey unknowingly gave Americans a self-rating system. Coincidental to this rating, but equally significant, Hugh Hefner's *Playboy* magazine taught men how to walk, talk, dine, and look like a superior sexual statistic. Men believed that they could move forward toward sexual security because they had, in the Hefner philosophy, a sexual mentor. Hefner was the Pied Piper who was expected to lead the way to a sexual wonderland of freedom.

If males were given a rating system and image, consider the effect on females created by the hourglass figures of the "can-those-be-real?" Playmates. The nude females conveyed a winsome combination of all-American, girl-next-door charms that, even when laid bare, expressed the congenial look-but-don't-touch aura that has become a trademark of the bunny clubs. In contrast to the virginal Miss America image of the 1950s, the Playmate ideal must have been a bit enigmatic for young females. Perhaps a public "no-no" but a private "yes-yes"?

Sexual reading thus had come out of the closet. People proudly displayed Kinsey's book and *Playboy* magazine on living room coffee tables. It was a visual sign of the sexual adroitness that went on behind closed doors. At least that was what we wanted thought about us.

By now you can begin to see how these two publications initiated a journey into the land of shared sexual self-ratings and self-images. The male wanted to see himself as a playboy with women: a devil-may-care soul who didn't take women seriously but who took them to bed frequently. The female, on the other hand, was a striking combination of innocent virginity and willing playmate. Her figure either flourished or floundered depending on the weight of her mammary glands, the slenderness of her legs and hips, and the winsomeness of a youthful smile. She was led to believe that, if she played her cards right, she could play sexual games and still not be considered a bad girl.

And so we walked hand in hand with the media down the primrose path toward what we thought was a sexual revolution. We didn't really change our behaviors: We merely became more "show and tell" about them. Ratings and images became a mania devoured by us, the public.

We wanted to read more, to see more, and to believe that a revolution was on its way. So the media willingly tipped its hat and told us that, indeed, we were in a sexual revolution. But did you think to ask, "Where is the revolution?"

THE PAST IS PRESENT

You talk revolution but live ancient history. Current sexual roles are neither new nor revolutionary. They continue to restrict, to limit, and often to define in inappropriate ways male and female sexuality. Participation in past images and interactions defeats newer, more positive, and less threatening relationships. Until you are free to make decisions about roles and images, the past is more influential than the present.

Living out past traditions while believing in a pseudo-sexual revolution is confusing. Yet many people live in this confusion. You may desire new ways of interacting, but strongly ingrained historical patterns are resistant to change. Let's examine some aspects of the problem.

The female's image throughout Western society has been, and continues to be, defined either by moral inferiority or moral superiority. One extreme or the other—the Seductress Eve or the Pure Virgin (more fully described in Chapter 5, "Your Sexual Heritage").

The male's sexual image is constant, whereas the female's image exists at one extreme or the other. The female is never on a par with the male—never his equal. She is unequal in sexual drive, responsibility for sexual actions, moral values, and self-concept. If one member of a relationship is not an equal, then neither person is equal.

Old double standard ideas hold fast. Notice the following double standard ideas that continue to establish who we are to each other and, especially, to ourselves.

Double Standard Roles

1. Females are responsible for saying yes or no to the decision to engage in coitus.
2. Females have less sex drive than males. The female, therefore, has less need for coitus.
3. Females who engage in premarital coitus are asking for trouble.
4. Males who engage in premarital coitus are "doing what comes naturally."
5. Females are more responsible than males for birth control.
6. Males must be experienced before marriage because they

are responsible for the sexual success or failure of the wedding night (and the sexual success or failure thereafter).
7. Females who "play around" are neurotics or nymphomaniacs, and they are also bad girls.
8. Males who "play around" are stable personalities.
9. Females who play around tend to be untrustworthy and hardhearted.
10. Males who play around tend to be dynamic, outgoing people who are sought after for their pleasant, well-developed personalities.
11. Males regard females who play around only as sexual objects, not as persons valuable for emotional involvement or support.
12. It is more serious for a female than for a male to engage in extramarital coitus because she is responsible for the happiness in the home and of the children. In essence, she is the guardian of morals.
13. Females who play around should not be allowed custody of the children in a divorce settlement.
14. Males who engage in extramarital coitus should not be ruled as unfit fathers on that basis.
15. Divorced males are worse parents than divorced females.
16. The greater the sexual experience, the less value given to a female.
17. The greater the sexual experience, the greater value given to a male.

As you can easily observe, these double standard ideas tend to discourage respect, trust, and honest communication. Why, then, continue to interact through such harmful images and roles?

A SEXUAL REVOLUTION IS...

By now you know what a sexual revolution is not. The more important question then becomes, "What is a sexual revolution?

What makes a sexual revolution?" As suggested earlier, a revolution changes, turns around, or reverses your thinking or acting. Different ways of interacting result. Here are some possibilities. You will instantly notice the improbability of these actually taking place.

Role Reversals

1. Males become valued for virginity until marriage.
2. Females are expected to "sow wild oats" before getting married.
3. Females assume economic and political power or control (imagine forty-nine female senators and one male senator).
4. Males view their primary concern as the home and children.
5. Males are given respect or disregard according to their chastity or lack of it.
6. Females are given stature according to their increasing number of sexual conquests.
7. Males frequently use coitus as a means of securing the relationship or ensuring marriage.

They do seem a bit absurd, don't they? Clearly, they are far-fetched. And the potential for more mutual and sharing relationships is equally far-fetched. You probably see the absurdity of these statements more easily, however, than that of the statements about the double standard roles.

Inequality is the underlying assumption of both sets of standards. Recognize that both lists are standards that define one sex as superior and the other sex as inferior. Both standards create unequal relationships, which, in turn, limit your choices for personal and interactional fulfillment.

There is yet another way of interacting: male and female equality. By equality I refer to sexual equality in responsibility, values, and concepts. Here are some examples.

Role Equalizations

1. Males and females are equally responsible for decisions to have coitus.
2. Males and females are equally responsible for the success or failure of coitus. (In actuality, these terms are competitive and don't belong in the bedroom.)
3. Males and females are not considered morally inferior or superior. Rather, they are morally equal.
4. Males and females accept each other as having similar sexual drives and needs.
5. Males and females have a single standard about premarital and extramarital coitus.
6. Males and females see each other as having comparable parenting skills and responsibilities.
7. Males and females view each other as individuals rather than as stereotypes.

Role equalization can lead toward a revolution that liberates, frees, and builds positive ways of interacting. It promises trust, not distrust. It allows you to go beyond the usual feelings that you shouldn't reveal either too much weakness or too much strength. It encourages sharing, not withholding or withdrawing. Which pattern of interactions do you desire? The double standard or the role equalization?

THE MYTHS OF THE SEXUAL REVOLUTION

When you accept the sexual revolution, you probably live certain myths of a pseudosexual revolution. The myths are many. And the more you participate, the more likely it is that you will feel sexually insecure. Let's examine several beliefs that may be currently causing you problems.

Having a Sexual Partner Says That I'm a Great Person

Having a sexual partner says nothing about you. Your personal liabilities and assets aren't derived by having coitus with someone. Even animals can copulate. And although it's nice to share in the pleasures, the lack of a partner doesn't say that your personality lacks appeal. If you grab someone to improve your status, you'll live to regret it when the doors close and the company goes home.

Notice too, our negative feelings about the single, divorced, or widowed person without a partner. In the pseudosexual revolution, a person without a sexual partner is a failure, a something-is-wrong-with-her or-him individual. Don't believe it. Why does having someone as an extension say that you therefore have a greater worth? It doesn't.

Don't allow yourself to get into a relationship for the wrong reasons. You are a person with value and merit in your own right. You don't need another person to make a statement about who you are. You may want a sexual partner, but remember that your personal worth, or lack of it, shouldn't come from having a sexual partner.

Changing Partners Is the Only Cure for Coital Boredom

How is going to bed with someone else going to help the relationship with your current partner? Eventually, if the relationship is worth continuing, you must go back and realize that one of you, more likely both, have become disenchanted with the bedroom antics. The sooner the problem is squarely faced, the sooner better coital experiences will occur.

It may simply be a matter of talking about your sexual fantasies, or it may require the guidance of a professional counselor to identify the nature of the problems. Know that changing partners to cure coital boredom only delays dealing with the problem. It offers few solutions.

The Pseudosexual
Revolution Liberates

The pseudosexual revolution does not liberate. It is a media-created phenomenon: The media need you to feel anxious and frustrated. Otherwise, you will not buy toothpaste, books, liquors, or beauty aids to alleviate your uncertainties.

In reality, the "liberated" message of the revolution commands that you jump on the conformity bandwagon. Conforming for the sake of conformity rarely liberates. Instead, it demands that you live by the choices of others.

Acceptance or rejection of coital behaviors must be appropriate for you. They should be decided upon because it's best for you—not because some distant executive has an idea to sell. Liberation is a personal phenomenon that can't be marketed like toothpaste.

Only the Young Are
Sexually Proficient

We live in a youth-oriented society that suggests that anyone over twenty-five or thirty is missing out, over the hill, a sexual has-been. These "senior citizens" over twenty-five must settle for second best or persuade some teeny-bopper to hop gleefully into the sack and share his or her potency with the Geritol set. And this is far less likely to be a possibility for "older" females.

Happily, the abilities and potentials of individuals aren't entirely based on age. Each age has benefits and drawbacks. For example, one positive aspect of the older male lover is his staying power. Oftentimes, an increase in age brings about an increased ability for prolonged coital activity. And females who have feared pregnancy frequently find greater enjoyment and excitement after menopause.

Don't sit and cry for yesterdays or wait and sulk for tomorrows. Today is yours. Don't limit your feelings of "sexual best" to any age. Thinking in terms of age and sexual prowess is silly. You are the age you are. Enjoy. Stop giving yourself reasons to bemoan what you can't change. Your ability to enjoy coitus is about ninety-nine percent psychological and only one percent physical. Well, put your ninety-nine percent to work for you. The one percent will follow.

Only the Beautiful Are Sexually Attractive

You see them in movies and on television. You read about them in books. They are enchanting and beloved. Their faces and bodies are perfection.

Where, you wonder, does that leave those of us who are merely mortal? Actually, it leaves us anywhere we want to be if we don't accept the pseudosexual revolution. When, however, you believe this media-marketed myth of the sexual revolution, you must try to become a cosmetically beautiful person in order to achieve sexual confirmation. Being beautiful doesn't give you a ticket to sexual or coital happiness. It makes you more easily noticed and initially, perhaps, more sought after. So what? People may buy a product for its packaging, but the product itself keeps the customer coming back.

If you don't happen to be Robert Redford or Farrah Fawcett-Majors, fifty people may not be lined up to whisper sweet nothings in your ear. But when you choose to feel good and positive about yourself and the way you look, that message attracts others. It makes them feel good to be around you.

There is an inner glow, a captivating spirit exhibited by people who like and accept themselves. You've seen people who weren't cosmetically beautiful, but you made way for them because they emanate an aura that plainly says they are important. Because they respect and feel their own uniqueness, they don't find it necessary to fill someone else's image of sexual attractiveness. There's a special beauty and charisma derived from believing in yourself.

*Everybody Is Doing It
2.5 Times per Week*

Your curiosity about statistics may create a need to conform to a standard and a proper number of times per week—a numbers game. But why should you care about national averages in the bedroom? One person's "not-enough" is another person's "too-much." Even partners cannot agree. One of you may be concerned that there isn't enough lovemaking, whereas the other person feels upset because it's too frequent.

There is no magic in the numbers, 2.5 or 3.5, and there aren't assurances that having coitus 2.5 times a week guarantees coital ecstasy. One time a month may curl your toes and be, in general, a euphoric experience. Or, for someone else, ten times a week may be just right.

Get out of the numbers game. Allow yourself to enjoy your own pace. Read the numbers and statistics if you must, but keep those facts and figures out of the bedroom.

*This Is (Isn't) Normal . . .
Uh . . . Isn't (Is) It?*

"Normal" suggests that more people do than don't or don't than do. That doesn't make it right or wrong, good or bad, pleasant or unpleasant, or successful or unsuccessful. It only says that someone somewhere believes it to be the norm. What is good or bad for others may not be appropriate for you. Coitus is like eating. Everybody has different preferences. What is steak and baked potatoes for one person may be beans and cornbread to someone else.

Be concerned with what the two of you enjoy rather than with what the various sex books say are clever and erotic movements and strategies. Naturally, each of you will have certain preferences and values that can be defined as normal. Sit down and talk about the things you like. Be willing to pleasure your partner as well as yourself. Certain of the things that are turn-offs simply relate to prior messages about whether it was a normal activity or interest. As long as you are considerate with each other, are not hurting each other, and are not selfish with each other, why be concerned with what is or isn't normal?

Males and Females Are Equal

We are, but we aren't. Talk, talk, talk. But very little action is behind the talk. Some people parrot the phrase, "Males and females are equal," because it sounds fair-minded, liberal, and revolutionary. They fear equality, but they talk about it anyway.

Inequality has often seemed more equal than equality. We grew up believing that males are more highly charged, and, therefore, we expect, overlook, and accept the male behavior, taking the nonchalant viewpoint that boys will be boys. Girls, however, should be ladies, and ladies are very much responsible for their behavior. We say, "Males and females are equal," but our behavior and attitudes suggest that "males and females are unequal," both in bed and out.

These eight myths of the sexual revolution are easily believed—but difficult to overcome. We rarely talk honestly about coitus or sexuality, and so these beliefs simply go on and on. How do you dispel something that you don't talk about? Frequently, myths are believed even though common sense tells you better. Examine some of them—you may decide to cast them aside.

SEXUAL DISORIENTATION, NOT SEXUAL REVOLUTION

We grew up believing that males are more highly charged, and, therefore, we expect, overlook, and accept the male behavior, exist, but males and females desire better ways to interact with each other. Yet new behaviors have not been firmly identified. From insignificant questions about who should open a door for whom to issues of greater consequence, the rituals and patterns are now indefinite. We are unsure about the who, what, when, where, why, and how of coitus. In many cases we are uncertain about whether the male or female career is more important in a relationship. We are even beginning to suspect that often times males make better single parents than females.

Unless you live in a vacuum, you will struggle with the how and whys of present and future sexual roles and behaviors. Traditional patterns are becoming less traditional. All around us, situations are changing: These changes change us. You may feel unsure about choices that twenty years ago would have been solidly defined for you. Unsureness often makes you feel guilty or anxious about transitional patterns and roles that you would like to assume.

The status quo exists, and yet it is changing. We still relate to each other through double standard communications. At the same time, the economic, political, and social environments around us are undergoing a metamorphosis. More equal legal and economic status is being gained by males and females. For example, females no longer have to remain at the bottom of the employment ladder. In another area, males are more frequently receiving alimony from females in order to continue being supported financially in the manner to which they have become accustomed. And those are only two of the many examples concerning the more equal legal and economic status of males and females. Look around you—the changing situations are plentiful.

But change doesn't mean that marriage and the family will become a forgotten unit, as some people fear. The desire for stability and commitment is too important to most of us. For every person who quickly moves from relationship to relationship, there are twice as many who stay for years in unsatisfactory relationships before getting out. Why? Because a successful male-female relationship is desired. The current frustration and disorientation, in part, reflects our efforts to bring about healthier, more complete patterns of relating. The rising divorce rates and the increasing numbers of couples choosing to live together don't seem to be saying goodbye to the commitment of marriage. Rather, these decisions are often rejections of unhealthy patterns of interacting that marriage encouraged in the past. The "Couples Syndrome," for instance, attempts to destroy each individual's personality after marriage in favor of the two people moving, thinking, reacting, and experiencing as one person. The very special qualities that brought them together gradually fade away in order to make them become a couple. The two unique individuals become a rather usual nondistinct unit or pair. Society sees them as John and Mary, not as John or Mary. They become their roles of husband and wife.

More males and females, however, are selecting not to play out the socially defined roles of husband or wife. Sometimes they avoid this role pressure by living together without the legality. Others have the legal paper but don't mold themselves into the set ways of interacting.

In this shifting period, you have the opportunity to do away with relationships that foster unhealthy dependences on each other—relationships where we grow to distrust, despise, and name call. The current period permits viewing ourselves as more fully functioning individuals who can give to another person—not in fear but by happy choice.

At this point in time, you may feel uncertain rather than liberated. The current sexual disorientation feels uncomfortable. Recognize, however, that through this discomfort personal and social growth can occur.

For most of us, the sexual revolution has not yet arrived. I am not telling you that this period of disorientation won't move toward sexual liberation. Indeed, I believe that we are going toward the most mutual, sharing, loving, and liberated relationships in the history of Western society. I believe that we are preparing to cast aside our games and half-truths and half-trusts of each other for more intimate relationships.

We are tired of the old, pointless games. We want better. We deserve better. And I believe we will have better.

Change is not easy. Change brings about stress, and we are certainly seeing that stress and discomfort now. But risking changes also brings about improvements. I believe that the disorientation that we now see is moving us toward respect, devotion, and mature love.

PROMOTING AN INTRAPERSONAL SEXUAL REVOLUTION

When you see that a sexual revolution has not yet taken place and you no longer accept the myths as the gospel, you have taken the first step toward promoting your own revolution. You are ready to accept yourself as special and unique, not as one to be directed by the fads and social whims of others. Although you live in a world of others, you can be free to be yourself. Know that you are a sensible individual—one who can make his or her own needs and wants known. You need not make decisions on the basis of either defending against a revolution or following the trend to behave as if there were a revolution.

Decide to have a private revolution. Think for yourself and establish your attitudes and behaviors according to the values that are most appropriate for you. Forget the myths of the sexual revolution. You are a worthwhile person, and you don't need to believe in a pseudosexual revolution to prove it.

SELECTED REFERENCES

Alston, Jon P., and **Tucker, Frances.** "The Myth of Sexual Permissiveness." *Journal of Sex Research* 9 (February 1973): 34–40.

Ard, Ben N., Jr. "Premarital Sexual Experience: A Longitudinal Study." *Journal of Sex Research* 10 (February 1974): 32-39.

Bauman, Karl E. "Selected Aspects of the Contraceptive Practices of Unmarried University Students." *Medical Aspects of Human Sexuality* 5 (August 1971): 76-89.

Bell, Robert R. "Sex as a Weapon and Changing Sex Roles." *Medical Aspects of Human Sexuality* 4 (June 1970): 99-111.

Berenbaum, Arnold. "Revolution Without the Revolution: Sex in Contemporary America." *Journal of Sex Research* 6 (November 1970): 257-267.

Bulter, Robert N., and Lewis, Myrnal. *Sex After Sixty.* New York: Harper & Row Pub., 1976.

Cox, Harvey. *The Secular City.* New York: Macmillan, 1967.

Davis, Keith E. "Sex on Campus: Is There a Revolution?" *Medical Aspects of Human Sexuality* 5 (January 1971): 128-142.

Delora, Joann S., and Delora, Jack R., eds. *Intimate Life Styles: Marriage and Its Alternatives.* Santa Monica, Calif.: Goodyear, 1972.

Freeman, Harvey R. "The Generation Gap: Attitudes of Students and of Their Parents." *Journal of Counseling Psychology* 19 (September 1972): 441-447.

Gagnon, John H., and Simon, William. "Prospects for Change in American Sexual Patterns." *Medical Aspects of Human Sexuality* 4 (January 1970): 100-117.

Glenn, Norval D. and Weaver, Charles N. "Attitudes Toward

Premarital, Extramarital, and Homosexual Relations in the U.S. in the 1970's." *Journal of Sex Research* 15 (May 1979): 108-118.

Hunt, Morton. *Sexual Behavior in the 1970's.* Chicago: Playboy Press, 1974.

Kennedy, Eugene C. *The New Sexuality: Myths, Fables, and Hang-ups.* Garden City, N.Y.: Doubleday, 1972.

King, Karl; Balswick, Jack O.; and Robinson, Ira E. "The Continuing Premarital Sexual Revolution Among College Females." *Journal of Marriage and the Family* 39 (August 1977): 455-459.

Kinsey, Alfred C. et al. *Sexual Behavior in the Human Female.* Philadelphia: Saunders, 1953.

Kinzel, Augustus F. "Impersonal Sex." *Medical Aspects of Human Sexuality* 13 (February 1979): 67-79.

Moulton, Ruth et al. "Sexual Responsiveness in Women." *Medical Aspects of Human Sexuality* 4 (January 1970): 53-65.

Petras, John W. *Sexuality in Society.* Boston: Allyn & Bacon, 1973.

Reiss, Ira L. *Premarital Sexual Standards in America.* New York: Free Press, 1960.

Robinson, Ira E.; King, Karl E.; and Balswick, Jack O. "The Premarital Sexual Revolution Among College Females." *Family Coordinator* 21 (April 1972): 189-194.

Scales, Peter. "Males and Morals: Teenage Contraception Behavior Amid the Double Standard." *Family Coordinator* 26 (July 1977): 211-222.

Thomas, Keith, "The Double Standard." *Journal of the History of Ideas* 29 (April 1959): 195–216.

Ward, Dawn and Balswick, Jack. "Strong Men and Vicious Women: A Content Analysis of Sex Roles Stereotypes." *Pacific Sociological Review* 21 (January 1978): 45–53.

chapter 4
MASCULINITY AND FEMININITY REVISITED

Once upon a time, you were an individual. You had your own thoughts and your own feelings, needs, emotions, responses, and desires. Then, after a very short time, you were made aware of the feelings, needs, emotions, responses, and desires of others. You were told, and you learned, to give up parts of yourself in order to please others.

If you were a little boy, you were told that you shouldn't cry, you shouldn't play dress-up, and you shouldn't be tenderhearted. You were supposed to be rough, strong, and unemotional. If you were a little girl, you learned to be emotional, dainty, and helpless. Because both little girls and little boys want to be liked, accepted, and respected, you did fairly much as expected.

Perhaps the sweet, demure little girl image or the rough and tumble little boy image didn't fit you at all. Nevertheless, you learned to fit an image that brought adult smiles instead of frowns. The smiles helped you feel warm, good, and loved; the frowns gave you cold, bad, and neglected feelings. For some of you, smiles came with little or no effort; for others, the task involved more failures than successes.

You learned as a little boy or girl many years ago to gain acceptance by conforming to the expectancies of others. By now, you can still visualize, deep inside, that little boy or little girl who wants acceptance very much. When you talk and act as people expect, they reward you with self-worth and self-esteem. The little girl or little boy inside you has learned that self-worth is gained by becoming masculine or feminine. Masculinity and femininity are socially determined values. Although the qualities of being male or female are biological characteristics, the qualities of masculinity and femininity are social judgments. These judgments affect your self-image and the images that others have of you. As you can see in the list that follows, masculine self-worth is associated with strength, whereas femininity is associated with weakness.

Feminine Self-worth	*Masculine Self-worth*
physically weak	rough
cute	aggressive
passive	competitive
helper	handsome
dependent	physically strong
dressed in frills	nonemotional
demure countenance	independent
acceptance from doing for others	worldly thinker
	acceptance through achieving for self
noncompetitive	
emotional	dominant
nurturing	fearless
follower	leader

To think of ourselves as needing to be entirely masculine or feminine creates a limiting, self-destructive quandary for ourselves and others. We are disappointed in ourselves and others when these unrealistic expectations of masculinity and femininty are not met. Those disappointments stifle honest, open communication.

Masculine and feminine images should not be superimposed or limited to one sex or the other. Unfortunately, however, these qualities have become stereotypes that most of us accept. We are willing to accept stereotypic images because they spawn certain images of self-worth. As we do so, we experience self-worth through judgments about masculinity and femininity.

MASCULINE AND FEMININE MYTHS

Generally, sexual myths are the ideas and images that are falsely believed to be biologically determined. You have been taught that altering these sexual images will tamper with the laws of nature.

Sexual myths include attitudes and behaviors related to work tasks, home life, recreational choices, child-raising responsibilities, interactions between the same sex and the opposite sex, and sexual intercourse. In other words, sexual myths and myths of masculinity and femininity affect every area of your life. And in all probability, you are currently participating in one or more sexual myths that keep you from personally satisfying interactions. Wayne and Susan, for example, were willing to sacrifice what, for them, would be a mutually pleasant life style because they believed the myth that a male's primary role is that of provider for his family. When Wayne and Susan first married, they both worked and willingly shared household chores, paychecks, and dreams. Three years later, they began having children: first, Andrea, and, seventeen months later, Jill. Susan tried staying home with the girls, but she found herself restless, grouchy, and moody. In their seventh year of marriage, after Susan returned to work, Wayne took a month's vacation to stay home with the girls, since

Susan had no vacation time available when Wayne was off. During that month, the house gained a beautiful sense of order that hadn't been seen since before the childrens' arrival. Meals were once again a delightful and positive time in the household. The girls were thrilled to have their father home, and Wayne loved every minute of it. Both Wayne and Susan were impressed with the peaceful and satisfying experiences during that month. They talked about trying, at least on a temporary basis, this rather unusual arrangement for a longer period of time. Their friends were appalled at the possibility. It wasn't as if Wayne were a failure at his job: He was an accomplished administrator at the university. Argument after argument was presented to the couple about the total absurdity of such a life style. Their friends could accept placing the role of fatherhood and housekeeping as a primary vocation. But that role was appropriate for a male who didn't have what it takes to skillfully earn a place in "the real world." It was, however, ridiculous for a successful man to make such a choice.

Slowly, the couple began to look at their plans as silly and surely unworkable. That was eight years ago. Occasionally, they think back to their rather frivolous idea and laugh. Yet today Susan has still not learned to coordinate mothering, housework, and time for herself, even though she is no longer employed outside the home. Wayne has continued to gain prestige and merit in his position, but he rarely spends any time at home with Susan and the girls. Instead, he has taken a mistress who allows him to relax in her apartment and feel comfortable just being himself.

Neither Wayne nor Susan is happy, but they have both committed themselves to live out what for them are myths of masculinity and femininity. They falsely believe that it is necessary to experience life according to an irrevocable pattern. Common sense would tell them to do what is best for their particular needs. But the myths of masculinity and femininity rarely permit common sense or personal needs to be a critical consideration. In living the myths, it becomes difficult to express needs, feelings, or life goals. You force yourself many times to forego your natural and spontaneous personality in order to become shaped into a masculine or feminine ideal. You may be giving up characteristics that are comfortable and suitable.

Remember, too, your frustrated and angry feelings when others don't respond according to your perceptions of sexual myths. Not only are you dissatisfied with yourself but you also become uncomfortable with others who vary from the acceptable range of images.

I am reminded of Jeannie and Morgan, who have been lovers for almost eight years. They do not live together and are very discreet about the sexual nature of their relationship. Still, the facts that they have, so far, selected not to marry and, as their friends have suspected, that they are indeed lovers, is a source of conscious curiosity and unconscious irritation. Jeannie's female friends have rarely said anything, but Morgan's male buddies make a continual round of jokes during their weekly poker games. The jokes are actually intended to gain information about the sexual state of their relationship and to learn why they don't get married.

Their friends don't recognize the actual level of their own interest. They feel threatened when Jeannie and Morgan are resistant to enter into the expected traditional marriage. We want others to behave as we do, which gives a seal of approval to our own choices. When people vary from us, particularly with respect to sexual choices, they threaten our own images. Jeannie and Morgan's friends would feel more comfortable if the couple made the same commitment, which in turn reinforces their own decisions. We can also see that certain of these individuals are probably not entirely comfortable with their own choices, and the constant reminder of Jeannie and Morgan's decision raises some questions about their own life situations. It is rather interesting that, although Jeannie and Morgan feel absolutely no need to defend their life style, their friends feel it necessary to do so. Part of the reason rests in the awareness that Jeannie and Morgan have made what appears to be a right life choice for them, even though it may be awkward for others. Certain of their friends, however, have chosen life according to the myths of masculinity and femininity.

This chapter offers you information about experiencing yourself as a freer, happier person. Begin to consider the masculine and feminine myths that interfere with the freedom to be yourself.

Change is not easy because it requires that you give up your need to conform. It means that you will take responsibility to become your own role model and that you must stop being the "ideal" of the super perfect hero or heroine.

You will not grow through adapting the images of other people. Attempting to become the image of someone else only creates a caricature of yourself.

If you accept the myths of masculinity and femininity, then you are not comfortable being yourself: You are trying to become someone else. In the process, you are losing your own special, distinctive, and unique qualities. Let's consider for a moment the young woman who decides to hide her intelligence by conveying an image of popularity and sexiness with males. In doing so, she loses a part of her real spontaneity and forces an image that could create cynical reactions and resentments about males. She has made a choice. She denies a natural ability that brings her many challenges and opportunities. In doing so, she attempts to change who she is for the myth of what she ought to be.

This, of course, is why we accept so unquestioningly the myths of masculinity and femininity. They establish who we should be, and they are well defined. Then we become unhappy about the effects of our sacrifices. Because we are interacting through myths, our communication is fake.

When we begin to feel uncertain about our own sexuality, we become hostile or manipulative toward the opposite sex. Remember this: You may be willing to bend, mold, and rethink your own personal needs in order to match the socially approved images, but you will never be totally comfortable living those myths. You will not be at ease and able to view yourself or others in a positive, confirming manner. You are not being yourself: You are a composite or, at best, a caricature of an image.

Carolyn is an example of just such a caricature. She has no time for friends, husband, or family. She believes that it isn't enough to be hard working, productive, and innovative. She thinks that it is necessary to maintain an image of being super tough and aggressive in order to keep both her bosses and those working under her somewhat awed by her tremendous power. If Carolyn believed in her own abilities and power, she could be pleased by her achievements and personal gains, but she is not convinced. And because she is not convinced, because she sees herself as a trembling, powerless little girl, she is "on stage" for eight to twelve hours every day in a role that leaves her emotionally exhausted. Then she collapses in the evening with a couple of drinks.

Talking to Carolyn about her difficulties is a matter of helping her to see that she has more to gain by giving up this image. It requires that she be able to understand that she need not sacrifice success by allowing people to see a bit more of who she really is. Carolyn is not the powerful, unfeeling demon that she attempts to play at work; neither is she a trembling little girl. There is a whole, beautiful person in Carolyn that contains both a little girl and a powerful woman. The more she accepts herself and works with people through an honest approach, the happier and more successful she is likely to be.

When Carolyn gives up playing a role, she can be successful in her accomplishments. She will enjoy the challenge of work and also make time for friends and relaxation. The image that Carolyn projects is, of course, unreal. Until she is free to release the myth she has created, she will continue to be unhappy.

Carolyn's need to find a balance between the weaknesses she fears and the power that she actually has is important. She has assumed certain characteristics of a role that are not compatible to her true nature or self; thus, those characteristics are difficult for her to maintain. But Carolyn is operating in a masculine arena, and she feels a necessity to assume qualities that are identified with successful men. This problem becomes less unusual as more women enter the business world as colleagues to men.

Certain life arenas are seen as masculine or feminine, but this does not imply that our behavior must be modified. It isn't necessary to adopt a role that is based on an unrealistic myth of sexuality. Make the most of your own characteristics. Be yourself—and live it!

You, like everyone else, are not totally strong or totally weak. Rather, you are a combination of strengths and weaknesses. See yourself as an individual. Don't try to squeeze yourself into predetermined masculine or feminine images; you may feel locked into a less than appropriate life style.

We have come a long way, for instance, from the nineteenth-century pedestal image of the female. That image was of a woman as frail, given to headaches, weeping, and fainting. She required constant attention and care from the father or husband. In many ways, we have discarded that image. Yet we continue to give the highest regard and personal worth to a woman whose image is beautiful and who needs to be taken care of. The "helpless" female personality is still perceived by some of us as making the male feel truly masculine. To teach one person to be dependent upon another is slavery in its truest form. Remove that caretaker from a person's life, and the ability to function is gone. Masculine and feminine interactions require that one person be dependent—the other independent; one weak—the other strong.

As for the contemporary male, who can doubt that our expectancy to see him as stronger and more powerful than the female has not significantly shortened his life? The pressures to obtain social status, career prestige, and monetary success take their toll on the contemporary male. He is told that to be masculine is to be fearless, to be the conquerer, to be a money-making machine. Masculinity demands too much. Let it go.

The acceptance of masculinity and femininity creates problems within the individual and sets up barriers between the sexes. Trying to live up to the images of masculinity and femininity does little to make male and female relationships comfortable or satisfying. Instead, the differences demanded establish communicative polarities. The age-old criteria, for example, that guys are out to get all they can, whereas gals must tease but never give in, sets in motion a game that neither sex feels very good about.

Remember that what we don't understand we tend to fear. In the case of stereotypic sexual images, there is an element of irresponsible and fake communication. Why can't we expect both persons to be responsible and honest about sexual feelings and needs? Responsible thinking tends to foster respect, whereas the acceptance of masculine and feminine myths will produce nothing more than misunderstandings.

Let's explore some myths of masculinity and femininity that you may be sexpressing. Several popular myths are described for you. Each statement is false. If you agree with any statement, it is because you are living that myth. In doing so, your interactions are limited to disappointments and frustrations when that myth is not met.

Read each statement and try to identify why you or others would accept and live through that particular idea. A great part of the power of myths rests in our willing acceptance of them. Begin thinking about these myths. Don't ask yourself whether you believe in these myths. Instead, ask whether it's something you choose to believe in.

1. Females are more romantic than males.
2. Males are more intelligent than females.
3. Males have stronger sexual drives than females.
4. Males are more self-confident than females.
5. Females are more emotional than males.

6. Males have greater emotional stability than females.
7. Females are more vain about their appearance than males.
8. Females have a greater capacity to give and receive love than males.
9. Males are more objective, logical, and direct than females.
10. Females are basically dependent, whereas males are basically independent.
11. Males are less interested than women in religion, art, music, and literature.
12. Males have a greater tolerance of physical pain than females.
13. Males are less concerned or hurt over the break-up of relationships than females.
14. Females have a greater need to be loved than males.
15. Females are more devious in their thinking than males.
16. Males should demonstrate no visible signs of fear or concerns with physical combat.
17. Females must choose between marriage and career; males should not have to make such choices. It is determined that the female should stay home and the male should provide for her.
18. A successful man can be measured by his income bracket.
19. Males must initiate sexual intercourse.
20. The prettier a female, the more acceptable she is.
21. Females should be flighty, scatterbrained, and childish; otherwise, they will threaten males.
22. Female minds are cluttered with small, insignificant things; male minds are filled with important, significant matters.
23. Females are soft-hearted and sentimental; males are hardhearted and insensitive.
24. Females are inferior to males. Males are superior to females.
25. The mother's role is more important than the father's role.
26. Females are not competitive.
27. It is the male's responsibility to provide complete financial support for his female and children.

28. The only way a female can find fulfillment is through her role as wife and mother.
29. The female personality is basically passive; the male personality is basically aggressive.
30. Females are more jealous and petty than males and engage in backbiting more than males.
31. Females who engage in premarital sexual intercourse or extramarital sexual intercourse are promiscuous, bad, and should be held in low esteem. Males who participate in similar premarital activities are merely sowing wild oats. Extramarital coitus in males is excused because they evidently have a sexually cold or maladjusted wife.

The acceptance of these ideas as appropriate creates a world of sexual expectations for yourself and others. Those expectations, when not demonstrated, cause an uneasiness inside you. You are not sure who the other person is when he or she varies from your expectations, and you do not know how to react.

Accepting these myths can short-circuit our thinking. We find ourselves and others boxed into narrow spaces. Our finer human qualities are strait jacketed, and we deny certain qualities that are needed. Varying situations require us to be aggressive or tender. Why, then, is tenderness a good quality in Jane but not in Richard? Why is aggression a positive characteristic for Richard but a personality fault in Jane?

Life is too complex to limit or deny half the existing emotions for either sex. Frequently, this limited range of emotion doesn't meet our needs. We find ourselves frustrated without knowing why.

Recently, an acquaintance of mine, while boarding his flight, offered to assist a woman with her luggage. Although a male rarely offers to carry another male's luggage, he frequently feels obligated to provide such assistance for a female. In this particular situation, the woman politely insisted on carrying her own luggage. My friend felt strangely embarrassed and made the short comment, "Oh, you must be one of those career women, huh?"

The first thing to understand is that my friend would not have been embarrassed if a male in a similar situation had not felt the need for help. Why, then, did he experience discomfort when a female turned him down? Why did his feelings of helpfulness and friendship turn to hostility? Because his limited range of sexual expectations was not adhered to. He went through the motions of being properly masculine, but the response received varied from his expectations. He wasn't allowed to be masculine. There was nothing in his background, in his stereotypic image of masculinity, to tell him how to react. He was not programmed to respond except through a limited and set pattern. Any deviation from his expectations creates an uncomfortable sensation, an uneasiness that must be dealt with by reacting to protect himself. His defense mechanisms rise to the surface.

The patterning of masculinity and femininity programs you to a limited range of comfortable and predictable interactions. Any unanticipated or unexpected variation brings momentary strugglings to regain personal confidence. When an unexpected response occurs, discomfort arises during that time of stress. You do not have the means to develop other appropriate responses. You are therefore left with nothing to fall back on except those limited patterns of masculinity and femininity.

When you are living through the ideal images of masculinity and femininity, any change in yourself or others will leave you uncomfortable. You are then moved to defend your structured belief. In so doing, your reactions tend to become hostile, sarcastic, angry, or hurtful. You may feel justified or prideful in defending your image of masculine or feminine behavior, but you have also interfered with the flow of interaction. In doing so, you may have terminated a positive friendship or exchange.

When, for example, women enter the work arena as colleagues, the interaction patterns are changed. Effective communication is stifled by the myths of masculinity and femininity. Men don't want to be harsh or unfair to women. However, they have been programmed only to deal with other men who compete or are threats to their careers. Men simply aren't sure how they might communicate with women who may be professional adversaries or peers.

We have been taught that masculine-feminine interactions are based on masculine superiority-feminine inferiority. When men do not get their expected response to a female through cute compliments or sexual innuendo, they don't know how they should act. Men have had little experience relating to women as competitive, intelligent equals. Therefore, a man attempts to return a woman to a position where he feels comfortable.

Let's refer again to my young friend who demonstrated proper masculinity at the airport. When the programmed action was not as expected, he became hostile because he wasn't allowed to be masculine. Situations may occur where you are not permitted to be masculine or feminine. Please understand, however, that other persons cannot keep you from being *male* or *female*.

The beautiful physical differences between males and females don't require that you severely limit life choices, needs, or emotions. You can distinguish this basic fact about masculine/male and feminine/female. You can also determine that it is not necessary to limit your experiences within the boundaries of masculine and feminine myths.

RITUALS OF MASCULINITY AND FEMININITY

There are many rituals of masculinity and femininity that we are expected to participate in and revere. We live by these rituals; our lives are patterned and set through rituals. Modifying these rituals isn't easy, because identifying rituals isn't easy.

Unlike primitive cultures that have ceremonies to announce one's arrival into manhood or womanhood, rituals of masculinity and femininity in our society aren't established in one ceremony or occasion. Instead, we prove ourselves again and again. The rituals described in this section don't promote self-growth or well-being. These rituals hinder your positive self-image.

There is a better way. Look at these rituals carefully; admit the dislike you feel for yourself or others for conforming to these rituals. Why not decide to give up these troublesome rituals of masculinity and femininity?

*The Rituals
of Masculine Superiority
and Feminine Inferiority*

Perhaps the most subtle and yet the most pervasive of rituals are those founded in masculine superiority and feminine inferiority. At the base of this attitude is the first and strongest ritual of masculinity: Males must prove at the earliest possible age that they are not feminine in any manner or thought. This ritual is played out by expressing dislike, intolerance, or disdain for any female dress, games, play, manners, expressions, or qualities.

Parents often make fun of or become angry with their sons when they exhibit feminine qualities. This can set in motion a negative attitude about females. The result of such attitudes enforces a one-up, one-down relationship between the sexes that becomes the great unwritten, but generally accepted, understanding that "males are superior—females are inferior."

*The Ritual of Masculine Brawn
and Feminine Beauty*

The athletic little boy with his strength, macho, and aggressiveness conveys the superiority of masculinity. Peers copy and defer to him, girls flirt with and adore him, and adults worship and acknowledge him. He learns the importance of power, strength, and winning. The ritual of masculine brawn is not simply the possession of strength. Rather, it is the continual demonstration and show of fierce, savage muscle that becomes not only a physical possession but, more importantly, a way of presenting oneself to the world through that image. The rituals of masculine brawn demand that it be proven again and again. No visible signs are shown that might be misunderstood as weakness. This restricts real needs and builds an inner rage that has to be released. Interestingly, however, when this frustration is not allowed expression, it explodes in a rage and is perceived as another proof of the ritual itself.

Little girls who are naturally pretty grow up to become beauties. They easily charm rivals and friends alike. The world belongs to such a girl. Peers copy her; boys run after her; adults make way for her. She is not, however, without fears. Prettiness is her major asset, and she knows that she must make the most of it. People enjoy looking at her, but they don't particularly care to hear what she has to say. She is not likely to be taken seriously. In order to prove herself anything more than a frivolous, charming, but sweetly stupid object, she must work twice as hard as her plainer sister. The plainer girl, on the other hand, learns that it is difficult to gain attention—and because she fights to be noticed, she is labeled as unpleasantly aggressive and competitive.

Women resent and feel uncomfortable about being labeled aggressive or competitive. This labeling has been reinforced by what mother distastefully called "tomboy behavior." And, what do mothers tell daughters about behavior? They tell them, "If you act like that, Daddy will be displeased with you, and the little boys won't like you."

*The Ritual
of Feminine Rejection*

Rejection is more than an abstract emotion to young women who are growing up: It is an image and also a feared experience. The constant threat is that males will not like them. They must always be on guard lest some male—almost any male—should reject them. The concern of rejection threatens females and influences many decisions and relationships. Women are not taught to be equally concerned about rejection from other females. They are, however, dependent upon male acceptance. When a female experiences even the smallest rejection by a male, she immediately feels "less than." She becomes "less than" because she has been taught to please daddy, uncles, boy friends, and all males, regardless of rank or social standing. If she fails to impress, please, or gain acceptance, she fights against the emotion of having failed, and she becomes "less than."

All are aware of this "less than" feeling. But rarely do they deal directly with this emotion. Instead, they invoke some coping behavior, such as laughing at themselves or laughing inappropriately. The emotions may be anger or hurt, but they stand and smile. Only later do they wonder why they laughed or smiled. This "less than" feeling can be countered by both male and female if the individual is willing to work at it.

Elaine experienced this "less than" feeling at least once a day. Most encounters with her bosses and, often, interactions with colleagues and friends left her feeling mentally smaller—that is, "less than." Criticism of any variety, regardless of how positively framed or constructive, would bring on that feeling. Sometimes it was simply being in the presence of someone who had more skills or information about a certain aspect or topic that would make her begin to feel "less than."

When Elaine and I started talking about her anxieties in dealing with other people, she did not recognize this "less than" feeling. She only knew that she often felt uncomfortable with people.

We started examining what body feelings she experienced at those times. For Elaine, it was a tension in her stomach. (For you, it may be a tightness in the chest or a clammy or flushed skin sensation.) Once Elaine identified the body sensation, we worked on the mental image that accompanied the body feeling. Elaine's mental image was that of becoming smaller than the other person, while the other person became larger and larger.

Once she identified the body feeling and mental image in these situations, she understood what was happening. When she realized that she made herself mentally smaller than the other person, she then dealt with the occurrence as it was taking place.

Elaine's reactions, when she was tense, became centered on how the other person saw her. Her thinking was almost completely "other-directed." Her own needs, thoughts, ideas, and information were diminished because she was concentrating so heavily on the other person. Gradually, Elaine was able to change her thinking and reacting from "other-directed" to "self-directed."

This "less than" feeling is found in both males and females. Rejection, however, is a ritual that is continually part of the feminine personality. It is more prevalent in females because they have not learned how to cope with the problem while growing up.

Remember, too, that because the female is taught so strongly to avoid male rejection, she reacts differently to males and to females. For instance, when a female superior reprimands a lower status female, the reaction may be direct anger or confrontation. However, if the female is reprimanded by a male, the feelings go much deeper and are more difficult to deal with directly or openly. She can cope better with rejection from another female because she has not been taught that rejection from another female lowers her self-worth.

If a male, however, becomes disappointed, angry, hostile, or negative in even the smallest way, he denies her feminine image. Male rejection of a female, even within the most insignificant interaction, is a powerful inhibitor. That power, even when expressed in a situation outside the framework of an intimate relationship, is hurtful. We can see, then, the effect on a woman rejected in close relationships with males.

The Rituals of Masculine Camaraderie

The assertion of sexual prowess is the basis for the rituals of masculine camaraderie. Sexual prowess, more than physical strength or size, exhibits the masculine sine qua non, the best of the best. If he does not convey an aura of sexual prowess, his status as a male is always in jeopardy.

The masculine challenge is a challenge to be a "man." It forms the arena in which a male lives. In the developmental rituals of masculinity, females are only an accessory; the challenge presented between males gives life its purpose. The challenge to be a man by one male to another either symbolically or directly puts him on the spot to prove himself. This proof may be power, fists, or sexual exploits. It is, however, his ability to prove sexual power with women that compensates for other shortcomings. Oftentimes, if his male companions believe that he lacks sexual ability with women, there is nothing that will raise his self-esteem with other males. These sexpressions between males, whether prefabrications, bravado, or myths, satisfy the challenge if they are somehow made believable. Many sexual myths get started or perpetuated in this manner. These sexpressions must be said with such conviction that males do, indeed, become convinced of the reality of even incorrect information.

The challenge is essentially this: "You don't know how to get a woman; and even if you did get one, you wouldn't know what to do with her; and if you did get one, you wouldn't be able to satisfy her." The last part of the challenge is particularly powerful, because the male is never sure whether this challenge to satisfy a woman indicates his lack of sexual mechanical ability or says that his penis is too small to do the job. There is only one answer for his defense. "If you think I'm no good, why don't you go ask Josephine." This works as a perfect solution for the ritual, because the male wins either way. If Josephine should for some reason indicate that he has indeed had sex with her, he wins. If she denies the charge, the male's response is simply, "That just goes to show you can't trust a girl—she will just lie to you."

The Ritual of Feminine Dependence–Masculine Independence

Often, women do not question whether a male relationship is good for them. Carla recognizes that her relationship with Joe is poisoned. Nevertheless, she continues in that relationship. Although she gets bad feelings about herself from that relationship, she won't put an end to it. And she fears that Joe may leave.

Males have the same feelings about breaking off a relationship with a woman who is bad for them. The difference is that our social attitudes teach that a female *needs* a male. We are taught to think of women as clinging vines who are nothing without a male to care for them. That image in stories, movies, and plays shows the most feminine and attractive women in these roles. Females grow up identifying with the suffering of these women. In fact, the ritual of dependency includes suffering. When a male "suffers," he becomes unmanly. When a woman "suffers," she exhibits the "soul of femininity." As demonstrated in real life and in the movies, the woman agonizes, writhes, moans, cries, and storms against the plight of her lost love. What does a male do in a similar predicament? Well, he sets that handsome square jaw against the forces of lost love and goes out to win a war or to amass a huge fortune. Hence, he wins back the heart of his love. In real life, because the male is taught the team spirit, he often says, "Win a few—lose a few." And before long, this rather brave statement so valiantly expressed to his male comrades becomes a very real emotion.

I am not suggesting that males suffer any less despair when rejected. This isn't true. But society encourages females to suffer, whereas males are encouraged to find another important experience in life, whether through work or in relationships.

Dependency, regardless of how cumbersome or troublesome to women, is considered a badge of femininity. As a sign of femininity, women continue feeling helpless without a male in their lives. It is a ritual that women learn—one that endears them to their daddies and male acquaintances. But it prevents and inhibits personal growth or a sense of self-worth.

The rituals of masculine independence are opposite to the rituals of feminine dependence. From early experiences, he is told, "Don't cry"; "Don't run away from a fight"; "Don't by a sissy"; "Don't be afraid." These messages attempt to make him tough, hard, and independent. Yet as he grows into adolescence and adulthood, these messages become a noose around his neck. If he is to have respect from both males and females, he must maintain a show of independence derived from masculine expectations.

The rituals of masculine independence must be experienced as a demonstration or show of independence: power, physical strength, financial success, and sexual exploitation. Attempting to develop or live these shows of independence creates difficulties in admitting fears, faults, or the need for emotional sharing. That male isolates himself in a prison that doesn't permit the expression of uncertainties or anxieties.

A powerful show of independence is presented by the male who does not develop caring relationships with women. He is considered the leader of the pack. His sexual independence is evidenced by the style, "Love 'em and leave 'em." His uncaring attitude toward women is designed to increase his desirability. For him, independence is a form of seduction. The male who plays out a show of independence selects either the totally dependent female or the totally independent female. Certain men need women to be completely dependent upon them. They use their show of independence as a power to bind them together. Conversely, other males fear females depending upon them. These men use their show of independence to isolate themselves from females. They relate to females who won't make too many demands. Men who play the show of independence don't want a mutual, sharing experience with women.

Another masculine independent image is set in sexpressions about the "simple life." In fantasy, he explores his need for a rustic life away from the survival efforts of this modern jungle. His life style, however, concentrates on working his way up the success ladder. All necessary means are invoked for attracting the attention of colleagues and superiors.

Inwardly, he isn't living the great, free, independent life that he views as so appropriate. He feels caught in the show of independence and believes that he is not truly his own person. Yet he will not fight to decide for himself what might bring peace and calmness into his experiences. His obligations to the wife and family stifle him. Even thinking about different life styles seems childish to him.

One of the greatest burdens to the contemporary male is the expensive house in the suburbs that he is told is his mark of success. That house, however, makes him stay in a job that he may fear or hate, yet he does not think that he should do any less for his family. He asks himself, "What kind of man would I be if I didn't give my family every possible advantage?"

Underlying his show of independence is an anxious awareness of an overriding fearful wall of passivity. This anxiety creates a stronger need to exemplify his show of independence to male comrades. Thus he closes off honest communication and friendship with other males. He believes that he must continue in the show of independence lest his male peers gain greater stature than he has. And males are taught that the "king of the roost" among males has an option of the best of females—including his own, if he is not showing significant strength.

We believe that the male is completely independent and free. Not true! His options change very slightly from childhood to adult messages. The childhood messages, "Don't cry"; "Don't run from a fight"; "Don't be a sissy"; and "Don't be afraid" evolve into adult rituals of power, physical strength, financial success, and sexual exploitation. He is still expected to perform as a "good little boy" for his wife, his boss, and his colleagues. He is given to understand clearly that any variation from the expected show of independence will be met with punishments that may disconfirm his manhood.

One such disconfirming wife was a pleasant and responsive sexual partner to her husband until he was not accepted into medical school—a dream she had personally sacrificed to make come true. Upon learning that he was not going to medical school and wouldn't be a prestigious physician, she refused to enjoy sexual relations with him again.

Many married men aged forty or fifty have long-term relationships with younger women. These women do not press males for expressions of the show of independence. They respond instead to qualities that he does not show to others, especially not to his wife. He tells this young woman his dreams, and she shares these dreams with him. Occasionally, one of these men will decide to give up all his amassed show of independence—the house, wife, and job—to run away with the woman who shares his dreams. And what do we think of such a man? We think that he is crazy. Why would he give up everything that means so much to us? How, we ask, can he be happy living such a life? It is difficult for us in our blinded state to understand that he has opted for true independence.

One of the greatest tragedies in modern life is that men—and their women—do not see the difference between the show of independence and the independent thinking and living that leads to a self-satisfaction.

OVERCOMING MASCULINE AND FEMININE RELATIONSHIPS

Do you want to have more meaningful and positive male-female relationships? Then give up your sexpressions that are set in the masculine and feminine images. Give up preordained images and dare simply to be yourself in these relationships. Risk asking others for what you really want instead of interacting through ploys that you believe have to be used to attract and keep a partner.

The masculine and feminine styles of relating are very much set in a kind of guessing, and if you expect people to guess what you need, you will always be disappointed. What makes you think that your partner can or should know what you want when you don't ask, when you are merely waiting and hoping that this person will magically know what you want and need?

Take the risk and tell people what you want. Dare to live your relationships to the fullest. Although this may sound easy, we keep locked within our heads a series of fears that can crush relationships. What are some of the inner messages that keep us from enjoying our male-female relationships? Try these on for size, and see how many you are hiding in:

1. I know he or she will leave me.
2. I know that he or she will stop loving me.
3. I know that he or she is better than I.
4. I mustn't let him or her know that I have certain anxieties about our relationship. I must keep those thoughts to myself.
5. He or she won't love me if I let him or her know who I really am.

Masculine and feminine styles of interacting help to harbor these fears. By their very nature, they inhibit honest, open communication. When you cannot talk freely and honestly, these distorted ideas set a certain tension that will erode the spontaneity and beauty in the relationship.

Sexpressions of masculinity and femininity do not bring trust to relationships. Instead, emotional insecurities are created between males and females. Don't build your relationships on insecurities. Recognize that your partner has the same needs for love, respect, trust, and honest communication that you do.

Let the spoken word set your anxieties free. Express your needs verbally. Listen to your partner's response and try to interact honestly. That is really important, and yet it is difficult for many of us. We can find the courage to express our feelings, but then we are anxious that the other person will not respond as we would like.

Begin to allow your partner to be himself or herself. Don't allow the myths, rituals, and expectations of masculinity or femininity to penetrate and spoil your relationship. Once you give up trying to control the other person and his or her responses to you, you can begin to take control of your own life again. You are then on your way to enjoying a fuller relationship.

You cannot control your partner; you cannot make that person react as you want; and you certainly cannot force another person to love you. What you can do is to experience your own life and its importance. Recognize that having that person in your life may add growth, self-awareness, and beautiful times, but realize that you are important in your own right, even if and when that person is not in your life. See that relationship as an added dimension to your life—one that you may choose to compromise at certain points in order to have that person in your life. After all, sharing life with another is what gives meaning to all other aspects of success, growth, and esteem. Make that relationship, if it contributes to your self-growth, a portion of your life that you willingly work to establish and enjoy. But do not see that relationship—and the need for that relationship—as having greater dimensions than your life without that person. Be free to love that person to the fullest. Realize the beauty of having that special person in your life. Rejoice in that love when you find it. But enjoy that love. Don't fear it. Don't let go because you fear hurt, rejection, hostility, and all the other negative emotions that keep you from being free to enjoy the rapture of the moment.

Be free to enjoy relationships and to give them a significant place in your life without fearing that your partner has a power to annihilate you. Then you become your own person. You will not be living through the myths, rituals, and images of masculinity and femininity. You will instead be free to participate and give in relationships because you are not a composite or a caricature of society. You will see your own special uniqueness, and that is the most powerful thing that you can experience and give to others.

SELECTED REFERENCES

Aaron, Ruth. "Male Contributions to Female Frigidity." *Medical Aspects of Human Sexuality* 5 (May 1971): 42-57.

Albrecht, Stan L.; Bahr, Howard M.; and Chadwich, Bruce A. "Public Stereotyping of Sex Roles, Personality Characteristics, and Occupations." *Sociology and Social Research* 61 (January 1977): 223-241.

Balswick, Jack O., and Peek, Charles W. "The Inexpressive Male: A Tragedy of American Society." *Family Coordinator* 20 (October 1971): 363-368.

Blumstein, Phillip, and Schwartz, Pepper. "Bisexuality in Men." *Urban Life* 5 (October 1976): 339-358.

Broverman, Inge K. et al. "Sex-Role Stereotypes: A Current Appraisal." *Journal of Social Issues* 28 (1972): 59-78.

———. "Sex-Role Stereotypes and Clinical Judgements of Mental

Health." *Journal of Counseling and Clinical Psychology* 34 (February 1970): 1-7.

Delora, Joann S., and **Delora, Jack R.**, eds. *Intimate Life Styles: Marriage and its Alternatives.* Santa Monica, Calif.: Goodyear, 1972.

English, O. Spurgeon. "How Do You Advise the Man Who is Overly Concerned About Female Orgasm?" *Medical Aspects of Human Sexuality* 7 (March 1973): 12-20.

Fasteau, Marc Feigen. *The Male Machine.* New York: McGraw-Hill, 1974.

Golden, Joshua S. et al. "Who Should Initiate Sexual Relations, Husband or Wife?" *Medical Aspects of Human Sexuality* 4 (February 1970): 34-45.

Greenson, Ralph R. et al. "What is the Psychological Significance of Various Coital Positions?" *Medical Aspects of Human Sexuality* 5 (February 1971): 8-16.

Herschberger, Ruth. *Adam's Rib.* New York: Harper & Row, Pub., 1948.

Kaye, Harvey E. *Male Survival: Masculinity Without Myth.* New York: Grossett & Dunlap, 1974.

Klein, Viola. *The Feminine Character: History of an Ideology.* 2d ed. Urbana: University of Illinois Press, 1972.

Komarovsky, Mirra. *Dilemmas of Masculinity: A Study of College Youth.* New York: W. W. Norton & Co., Inc., 1976.

Korda, Michael. *Male Chauvinism: How It Works and How to Get Free of It.* New York: Random House, 1972.

Litewka, Jack. "The Socialized Penis." *Liberation* 18 (March-April 1974): 16-25.

Millman, Marcia. "Observations of Sex Role Research." *Journal of Marriage and the Family* 33 (November 1971): 772–776.

Naffziger, Claudeen C., and Naffziger, Ken. "Development of Sex Role Stereotypes." *Family Coordinator* 23 (July 1974): 251–258.

Rudy, Arthur J., and Peller, Robert. "Men's Liberation." *Medical Aspects of Human Sexuality* 6 (September 1972): 84–93.

Ward, Dawn, and Balswick, Jack. "Strong Men and Vicious Women: A Content Analysis of Sex Roles Stereotypes." *Pacific Sociological Review* 21 (January 1978): 45–53.

Yachnes, Eleanor. "Some Mythical Aspects of Masculinity." *Medical Aspects of Human Sexuality* 7 (September 1973): 200–215.

Young, Rosalie F. "Current Sex Role Attitudes of Male and Female Students." *Sociological Focus* 19 (August 1977): 309–323.

part two
Sexpressions:
SOCIETY AND YOU

chapter 5
YOUR
SEXUAL HERITAGE

If you assume that sexuality is a small, inconsequential part of your world, you are mistaken. All communication is sexual. Yes, all communication is sexual. You live in a world that is totally sexual. The world is comprised of males and females. You act and react according to your gender. As a male or a female, you are seen, heard, and touched in a certain fashion. In a word, you communicate on the basis of your sexuality. Are you threatened by that sexual fact, or do you enjoy it? Sexuality can be negated, despised, rejected, or enjoyed, but it nevertheless remains a most important factor in your identification. Why not learn to enjoy this really fine arrangement of life? Why not learn to say, "Vive la difference?"

Every minute of your life is shaped by your experiences as a male or a female. So what? Well, it is indeed critical for you to look at the sexual role that you have inherited. It is, after all, the primary means by which you address the world and are, in turn, addressed by the world. You may live, work, and play more comfortably once you understand the heritage of maleness and femaleness.

YOUR SEXUAL HERITAGE

You may wish to tell me that sexual attitudes are changing. Yes, they are—in a fashion. But let us not assume that sexual values and attitudes will be shed as simply as taking off clothes. You live in a world of others, and sexual concepts are the foundations of society. The messages you collect, store, and experience about how males and females should behave influence every aspect of your life. Your acceptance of sexual roles and coital participation molds your personality, but these roles and coital participations also form and control society. Decisions about sexual roles determine family design, social structure, and self-images for males and females. It is, of course, the things we are taught by our families that provide the backdrop for these decisions, which establish the division of work roles, political interests, child raising, appropriate play activities, and the regulation of coital activities.

It's hard to believe that we have something in common with our ancient ancestors, yet your sexual life style, activities, and attitudes have been socially practiced for centuries with very little change. The sexual and coital roles you experience are communicated from generations past. You tend to think of your sexual attitudes and behaviors as exclusively your own. In actuality, sexual life styles have been adopted by you from the society in which you live. Having a greater awareness about historical influences can help you to determine—to a greater extent than ever before—your own sexual personality.

This awareness will begin as you follow along in the next few pages through a description of three important historical sexpressions. These historical sexpressions reach out and affect your current attitudes and interactions. Your self-image and the images of the opposite sex are fostered in and by your acceptance of these basic sexpressions. Centuries ago, and today as well, female and male relationships are played out through the following: the double standard, images of woman as a Seductress Eve or a Virgin Mary, and romantic communication.

THE DOUBLE STANDARD

In our society today, we have one standard of coital activity for males and a totally different standard of coital activity for females. These standards greatly influence our thinking and are popularly referred to as the double standard.

Acceptance of the double standard mandates a remarkable difference in coital activities for males and females. The standard for males permits—and generally expects—participation in premarital and extramarital coitus. Esteem and self-worth are increased when a male dabbles in coital escapades. The coital standard for females, however, is quite the opposite. Females are advised to save their virginity for their husbands and always to pledge him faithfulness. The same indiscriminate coital activity that is often admired in the male brings disrepute to the female.

You may believe that the double standard no longer exists and that it no longer influences us. This is a prominent misconception. Actually, this system of relationships is still very much a part of your expectations for male–female interactions.

I recently saw a strong example of double-standard thinking. Because I was new in town, a married couple was showing me the sights and certain people's homes. At one point, the husband's voice became harsh as he told me, "My best friend dated the girl who lives in that house." He continued, "I tried to tell him that she puts out for every guy in the area, but he wouldn't listen."

Did I ask why sleeping around was all right for his buddies but immoral for a female? No, I didn't, because people who are double-standard thinkers are not likely to accept a single standard. Most of us are not ready to accord the same coital privileges and experiences to males and females. And for most of us, this probably does not strike us as being anything beyond "how things are." We do not question why things are as they are. We don't consider that there may be a better way of relating.

The double standard applies primarily to coital practices. Yet it inherently sets forth the corresponding attitudes of male superiority/female inferiority that then extend to the more general female and male relationships. When you accept the double standard, can you see that you provide a privilege to one sex while denying that privilege to the other? When a privilege is granted one sex and denied the other, the double standard sets up a barrier of anxiety between males and females. The male is accorded a dominant, superior status. But nothing arrests the sexual anxieties that accrue to that position. Such a superior position suggests, and rather plainly demands, that males see themselves as more knowledgeable, more skilled, more highly sexed, and always in control of the coital situation. Superiority implies being "greater than," whereas inferiority implies being "less than." The double standard contributes to a male's anxieties about impotency by requesting a larger than life performance. Conversely, the female's "less than" image convinces many women of their lesser ability to have regular orgasms or enjoyment. Greater than—less than: a double standard. The results? Misunderstandings, as well as dishonest and debilitating sexpressions.

Acceptance of the double standard sets up a real barrier between the sexes that creates a myriad of expectations. Such expectations can eliminate sexual sharing entirely. The double standard nourishes and feeds the anxieties that males and females presume about each other.

Giving up the double standard leads toward mutuality of expression and understanding. It breaks down walls of defensiveness, guilt, hostility, and distrust. It eliminates the need to play games. Clearly, it is impossible to accept the double standard and simultaneously experience male–female mutuality.

How is it, then, that such a troublesome system of relating has become so firmly entrenched? Let's go back to our heritage for explanations. Did you know that although the double standard was not practiced in all cultures, it was evidenced in Western civilization as far back as the ancient Hebrew, Greek, and Roman cultures? Actually, the perpetuation of the double standard was an advantage for those who set it as a base in early Western civilization.

Property rights of the male to his females was one of the earliest concepts that gave power to the double standard. This, in turn, established the male superiority/female inferiority relationship boundaries that have been so strongly accepted. The male's power was absolute; he had the power of life or death over his females. Women were killed by disgruntled males for deeds ranging from taking the wine keys to participating in, or even being accused of, adultery. The female belonged to the male. She was his property and lived in total subjection to him. He was superior; she was inferior.

Males owned their females. Females were the male's chattel; and, so bound to him, a female knew little beyond the treatment, attitudes, and behaviors shown by the particular male with whom she lived. It naturally followed that, since she belonged legally, religiously, physically, and emotionally to the male, she was certainly not in a position to compare the male's coital performance. The potential for male competition was, in most cases, effectively avoided. And after all, which of us wants unnecessary competition if we can avoid it? Human beings are rather like that, wouldn't you say? Males don't have the market cornered on anxieties. However, at that time, they had power to take certain action against their anxieties. I must admit that if the situation had been reversed, women probably would have behaved as did men.

Also important is that most Western societies thought that only males possessed a sex drive of any consequence. This established a biological imperative that supported ethics for the double standard. This biological imperative reasons in the following manner: "Aha! If a woman does not have a biological motivation or excuse for premarital or extramarital adventures, for her to engage in such activities presumes that she is, indeed, a corrupt, bad individual." At the other extreme, both sexes understand that the male is privy to such encounters because of his need to obtain coitus.

Another rationale for the double standard is identified with the paternity of a child. Determining the legitimacy of a child was of considerable importance, particularly in Hebrew teachings. Linked with the religious affirmation, and equally vital, was the male's need for emotional assurance about fatherhood. Naturally, no clear-cut procedure exists, or ever has, to establish absolute paternity. The only assurance of fatherhood was to isolate females from other males and to impose serious consequences on women who dared break the rules of the double standard.

The double standard was unquestioningly adhered to in most cases. The total effect of the double standard's acceptance is forcefully demonstrated in early Christendom. The Church fathers were anti-female. They were so openly opposed to and fearful of women they by A.D. 595 the Council of Macon was the center of a heated debate to decide whether or not women should actually be considered human.

The double standard was not solely to the advantage of males. In exchange for the female's acquiescence, certain economic and emotional supports were given her. Not the least of these supports was the assurance that, although females were certainly not equal to males, the "good" female (that is, one who faithfully accepted and kept the double standard) was at a higher social level than the "bad" females. This provided a hierarchy among women whereby they might have an identity of their own rather than one completely centered on the social or economic achievements of their mates. Although the female's status was often diminished in comparison to that of the male, acceptance of the double standard permitted a powerful pecking order among women. Notice that, even today, the double standard is more firmly accepted among women whose lives are lived through their husbands or fathers. Women who form their own identities tend to reject the double standard. For the female, keeping the double standard assured her of a certain social position and rank among both males and females. Her male did not have to risk coital competition among other males, and he could also be assured that his female's children were, indeed, his own.

Perhaps the only difference between historical and contemporary regulations of the double standard is the manner of punishing those guilty of trespassing the rules. Historically, the punishments for sexual transgression were often physical abuses ranging from beatings to death. In the past few centuries, the punishments have become increasingly psychological, and we continue today to allow these psychological factors to influence male and female behavior.

Today, the coital double standard is beginning to lose acceptance: It is an aspect of sexual interactions that many males are willing to give up in favor of more sharing relationships. At the same time, the male's ability to control his sexual environment by way of the double standard is an extremely powerful weapon. It is important for you to recognize the security that is built into this way of experiencing the sexual world. When you begin to grasp the strong sense of invulnerability that is derived from the double standard, you can see that it is not easily given up. We tend to think that giving up the double standard in favor of sexual equality means that sexual promiscuity will follow. Instead, there is evidence that the opposite is true, and we find that although males and females may be more open about the sexual activity that they are choosing to engage in, there is no evidence of increased promiscuity. As the validity of the double standard is questioned, there is evidence from research that brief sexual encounters are being rejected in favor of more caring, ongoing relationships.

Yet we are not comfortable with each other. We have not

learned to develop honest, trusting sexual communication. So we continue to reside within the familiar context of our double standard sexpressions. In doing so, we continue to build walls, not bridges.

SEDUCTRESS EVE— VIRGIN MARY COMMUNICATION

As we have seen, woman in Western society has been regarded throughout history as one extreme or the other—totally good or totally bad. The seductive nature of woman as personified by Eve is viewed as negative, bad, sexually inferior, and corrupt; whereas the image exemplified by the Virgin Mary is held as positive, good, sexually superior, and chaste. Never has the female been considered morally equal to the male, and never has she been granted the same coital rights as are accorded to the male. Rather, sexuality has been a device to control woman's place in society. By conforming to either sexual image, she has identified and objectified her sense of worth. Women are left to decide what to do sexually and then to accept the consequences. This tends to initiate a self-fulfilling prophecy. Her acceptance of one of the images sets the stage for rewards and punishments.

Let's explore more fully the image of the Seductress Eve. Think again about the story of Adam and Eve. In that story, Eve tempted Adam. Although this temptation was certainly not an inducement to coital pleasure, the sexual implications have not been overlooked. Moreover, throughout Biblical writings, woman was viewed as a seductress. Man had to be on guard against her sexual charms, her beauty, and her ability to overthrow his sensibilities. And being on guard against another individual doesn't make for very affectionate relationships, does it?

Eve, because she was a creature so easily tempted and because she, in turn, tempted Adam, then found herself in subjection to Adam. Because of her supposed sexual nature, woman has been perceived as requiring to be watched and guarded. Man, conversely, has not been responsible for his sexual actions because the nature of woman drives him into a sexual frenzy.

Different cultures have regarded female sexuality in various ways. The Hebrews, for example, recognized the female's sexual drive. They believed that it was necessary to care for and attend to those coital needs, even to the point of expecting the husband to attend to the coital needs of wives and concubines before leaving on a trip. The Hebrew's acceptance of the female sexual drive is in direct contrast to the early Christian denial of female sexual urges. Partly because Christianity sprang up in the Greek and Roman cultures where coitus was practiced with few moral constraints, early Christians soon placed chastity high above coitus. A measure of one's devotion and dedication to Christianity was the ability to abstain from coitus, even within the bounds of the conjugal bed.

Church fathers did not want to look at their own sexual nature; instead, they concentrated on their anxieties about female sexuality. The shameful nature and image of women was a constant theme for the early writings of the Church. Tertullian, for example, in the second century A.D., called women the gateway to hell.

Consider the impact on both males and females who were influenced to believe that women were inferior. Recognize also that there was little opportunity for women to acknowledge or express frustration with this role in society. And these negative attitudes toward women were passed down for centuries without interference. It was accepted that women were inferior to men. Also, it was believed that women were responsible for the sexual frustrations that men were feeling. Yet the attitude that women are, and always have been, the guardians of morals has been handed down through Western civilization with little or no resistance. Doesn't that strike you as a rather strange double bind? On the one hand, she is to be watched and subjugated, and on the other, she is to guard her own morals and by so doing protect the morals of the male. A rather strange situation, wouldn't you say? Her sexual nature placed her in a good-bad dichotomy.

This good-bad woman dichotomy has been consistently accepted throughout Western history. The American experience firmly established the image by the 1800s: good and sexless or bad and sexy. Nineteenth-century males could barely tolerate "good" women who showed even a small interest in sexual drive or passion. This good-bad woman continuum was more severely experienced at this time than at perhaps any other time in history. Brides were admonished not to move in the marriage bed. They were told that coitus was a duty to be tolerated. Husbands, they were informed, knew how indelicate coitus was for women and how faint of heart females were about such matters. Naturally, the male would never ask to see the female body, and in order to respect the female, he would complete the "dreaded" act as soon as possible. Foreplay was unthinkable.

Women who did possess interest in their bodies, or those who showed any enjoyment in coitus, were treated for this unusual ailment by the family physician. Various treatments were designed to remedy females of their perplexing and abnormal condition—the most horrendous treatment being a clitoridectomy (surgical removal of the clitoris). Women were thus programmed by society to deny their natural sexual drives.

A certain anxiety was also passed to the nineteenth-century male. He was made to understand clearly that only so many ejaculations were possible—the exact number was not foretold. Engaging too often or too many times would cause all manner of psychological and physical illnesses. Many problems seen in infants and children were also believed to result from too many ejaculations. Mental retardation, consumption, and girl infants were just a few of the many fates in store for the male who had experienced too many climaxes.

Attempts to conserve his sperm reinforced the need for a sexual scapegoat. Rather than consider his own sexual nature, he placed the responsibility on the female. The images of woman as Seductress Eve or Virgin Mary strengthened her role as a guardian of morals. She was supposed to be the hallowed wife-mother. Anything less than that pedestal image—that is, any sensuality in the female—indicated that she was bad and was leading the male toward his physical and emotional downfall. As guardian of morals, she was not only responsible for containing her own feelings but was especially to blame for any desire kindled in the helpless male. She was not a "playmate" to her husband.

These attitudes and behaviors, which work to defray the male's anxieties and also cause the female to shoulder all the responsibility, create communicative walls between the sexes. Such differences in sexual responsibility bypass the potential for males and females to relate in a sharing, mutually intimate, and maturing relationship. It does so because both expect the female to bear total responsibility for any bad feelings, anxieties, or boredom that are derived from sexual intercourse. That is, since the female is morally responsible for the decision to allow the act of coitus, the male then becomes free from blame or consequence. Although we will see in Chapter 10 that the contemporary male is now certainly responsible for a great many technical aspects of coitus, he nevertheless remains basically blameless for the initial decision, which carries the implications of moral turpitude with it.

ROMANTIC COMMUNICATION

Love, sex, and marriage have not always been considered prerequisites for ideal relationships. For hundreds of years, marriages were initiated, formed, and experienced on the basis of family agreements, social status, and other nonintimate considerations. The trend toward more amorous and fanciful reasons for relationships was brought about by several factors.

The Church fathers set the Doctrine of the Immaculate Conception in the fourth century. As we have seen, this virginal image stressed by the church represented the ideal role and place of the female in the world. The Church was actually having little success, however, in convincing the masses that this was indeed the proper image for woman, particularly because the Middle Ages were times of such raging moral corruption. In the twelfth century, small groups of troubadours strengthened the virginal image. Their poems and songs praised the virtues and beauty of the ladies of the manors. As these men went throughout Europe, the exquisite picture they portrayed raised woman's position to a pedestal high above that of man. For centuries, woman had been viewed with little respect or esteem; this new image placed her far above the mundane, everyday existence. Knights of the castles were exhorted to do valiant deeds and great battles for these ladies— and merely for the touch of a hand or the lady's ribbon. This was called courtly love and was *said* to be above the physical realm.

This was not a time when love, sex, or marriage were in any way related; couples married for prestige or social position, not for love or sex. The fanciful aura initiated by the troubadours raised the image of woman to a new purity and grace. During the following centuries, amorous love would affect the relationship between husband and wife, creating a different way of communicating. As the romantic infatuation became more central to female-male relationships, the value of sexual attractiveness increased. The female's value became wrapped in her ability to attract men, both as a sexual object and as a prized possession.

The impact of amorous love in our own society has been tremendous. From adolescence on, males are attempting to talk and act in ways that convince the female that they are sexually inclined and overwhelmed by her charms. The higher the value a male places on a female, the more ardently he pursues her. Conversely, the lower the value a male places on a female, the less effort he makes to convince her that he is enthusiastically involved. Also, the more a male views a female in a negative sense, the less energy he exerts toward an ardent courtship. The more he sees her as valuable, the more he attempts to indicate his infatuation.

Because we stress passionate love so strongly, we have developed a need for the childlike, super-real fantasies to go on and on. We depend upon that initial glow to tell us that life has meaning and is worth living. When the original passion fades, we no longer view the relationship in a positive way. We become restless in the relationship and look for a means to extricate ourselves from an experience that does not continue to make us feel ten feet tall. Our quest and belief in passionate infatuation moves us beyond reality into a continual search for utopian fantasy. When this euphoric elevation with our partner begins to subside, we don't wish to see ourselves as merely mortal. So we move on in search of another person who will momentarily see us in greater than real life dimensions.

Because we see the opposite sex often as god more than as mortal, we have become overly concerned with cosmetic appearances. We have convinced ourselves that being more than human disallows such human factors as getting fatter or older or having anything less than a perfectly proportioned body.

Our quest for the amorous ideal makes us less than human instead of more human. We tend to be less accepting of ourselves and others because we seek the impossible: perfection. And perfection is an unattainable image. Our communications to ourselves and to others will be set in frustrations because they come from messages determined from perceived infatuations that strive for perfection.

HISTORICAL SEXPRESSIONS AND YOU

The sexpressions of the double standard, woman as either a Seductive Eve or a Virgin Mary, and romantic communication are part of your culture and language, and they do indeed influence you and your sexuality. Whether you are a male or a female, the strong messages received about these ideas create anxieties that inhibit free and sharing male-female sexpressions. Although you may not be conscious of certain images, in truth, the series of messages are so entrenched that you probably don't notice them.

Your heritage through centuries past and your present experiences have instilled in you many messages about male-female sexuality. Can you now begin to see those influences? Your acceptance of the double standard, woman as either a Seductress Eve or a Virgin Mary, and romantic communication set the stage for your sexual interactions. In many ways, those messages from your heritage have been reinforced by the sexual information sources of parents, peers, the media, and sex experts.

SELECTED REFERENCES

Bailey, Derrick Sherwin. *Sexual Relation in Christian Thought.* New York: Harper & Row, Pub., 1959.

Beigel, Hugo G. "Romantic Love." *American Sociological Review* 16 (June 1951): 326–334.

Bullough, Vern L., and **Bullough, Bonnie.** *The Subordinate Sex: A History of Attitudes Toward Women.* Baltimore: Penguin, 1974.

Calhoun, Arthur W. *A Social History of the American Family from Colonial Times to the Present.* 3 vols. Cleveland, Ohio: Arthur H. Clark Company, 1917.

Cole, William Graham. *Sex and Love in the Bible.* New York: Association Press, 1959.

Doniger, Simon, ed. *Sex and Religion Today.* New York: Association Press, 1953.

Frazee, Charles A. "The Origins of Clerical Celibacy in the Western Church." *Church History* 41 (June 1972): 149–167.

Graves, Robert, and **Patai, Raphael.** *Hebrew Myths: The Book of Genesis.* New York: Doubleday, 1963.

Hogeland, Ronald W., ed. *Women and Womanhood in America.* Lexington, Mass.: Heath, 1973.

Hunt, Morton M. *The Natural History of Love.* New York: Knopf, 1959.

Lawrence, Henry W. *The Not-Quite Puritans.* Boston: Little, Brown, 1928.

Lea, Henry C. *The History of Sacerdotal Celibacy in the Christian Church.* New York: Russell and Russell, 1957.

McNamara, JoAnn. "Sexual Equality and the Cult of Virginity in Early Christian Thought." *Feminist Studies* 3 (Spring-Summer 1976): 145–158.

May, Geoffrey. *Social Control of Sex Expression.* New York: Morrow, 1931.

Patai, Raphael. *Sex and Family in the Bible and the Middle East.* New York: Doubleday, 1959.

Riegel, Robert E. *American Women: A Story of Social Change.* Cranbury, N.J.: Associated University Presses, 1970.

de Rougement, Denis. *Love in the Western World.* New York: Pantheon, 1956.

Rugoff, Milton. *Prudery and Passion.* New York: Putnam's, 1971.

Scott, Anne Firor. *The Southern Lady: From Pedestal to Politics, 1830–1930.* Chicago: University of Chicago Press, 1970.

Taylor, G. Rattray. *Sex in History.* London: Thames and Hudson, 1953.

Taylor, Peter L. "'Denied the Power to Choose the Good': Sexuality and Mental Defect in American Medical Practice, 1850–1920." *Journal of Social History* 10 (June 1977): 472–489.

Walters, Ronald G. *Primer for Prudery: Sexual Advice to Victorian America.* Englewood Cliffs, N.J.: Prentice-Hall, 1974.

chapter 6
PARENTAL SEXPRESSIONS

Find them in a tree or under a cabbage leaf. Buy them in a supermarket or hospital. Request delivery by a stork. You probably know what these have in common. They are examples of the facts of life as told to children by parents.

Sex is basic to life. Yet the facts are rarely discussed in an honest, open, and unembarrassed manner. Parents dread the time when they may be called upon to answer sex questions. In part, that apprehension comes from what they know and what they don't know. They know that males and females have different physical equipment. Beyond that, heaven only knows what strange information is attached to the "basics."

If parents have been a bit puzzled by the information, how can they clarify such things to a half-pint five-year-old, much less a gangly thirteen-year-old?

Cheer up. It isn't as bad as you think. We're going to explore some of the reasons why you may be afraid to talk about sex and we are going to take the starch out of those fears.

Think back on your own sex education. Was the information generally accurate or inaccurate? Fact or fallacy?

Positive or negative? Who provided most of your information? Although we tend to believe that parents are the primary source for education, this isn't generally true. Parents are the best source, but they aren't the major source. For most people, friends provide the most information. Consider your own experiences by responding to these seven true-false statements.

My parents or parent taught me the following:

1. The correct names of the male and female sex organs. TRUE ____ FALSE ____
2. About pregnancy. TRUE ____ FALSE ____
3. About birth control methods. TRUE ____ FALSE ____
4. About masturbation. TRUE ____ FALSE ____
5. About menstruation. TRUE ____ FALSE ____
6. About the emotional aspects of male-female relationships (in discussions, not lectures). TRUE ____ FALSE ____
7. That sexual intercourse is a positive, pleasure-giving act. TRUE ____ FALSE ____

You probably didn't answer most of these statements by checking "true." Actually, few people receive much direct or positive information from their parents. And I can probably demonstrate how little this situation is changing. Read over the statements once again. This time, check to see whether you provide that information to your own children. You may be surprised that these statements reveal how little you have told your children about sexuality.

Unless you are a single parent, you may hope that your partner will supply the necessary facts. That may or may not be true. In reality, whether you are a mother or father and whether your children are sons or daughters, the responsibility is yours. It can be an opportunity, not a burden. Talking about sexual ideas is another way of building rapport with your children. It can add another caring and respectful dimension to the relationship.

You know that discussing the facts of life with children is important. In fact, you probably grew up thinking that you would talk more with your children about sexuality. Why haven't you?

When parents talk openly and honestly with their kids, at least four positive predictions can be made:

1. Children grow up comfortable and pleased with their bodies.
2. Children are more likely to make their own sexual decisions, rather than making decisions based on the behavior of peers.
3. Children attain greater respect for the opposite sex.
4. Children attain a more positive attitude about coitus and generally find it enjoyable and pleasurable.

I cannot promise that these four benefits will naturally follow when parents are open, honest, and sensitive with their children about sexual matters. Yet the potential for positive attitudes and behaviors seems more likely than if a child receives sparse or negative information. Why not, then, take the time and effort to communicate more effectively with your children?

THE AWKWARD TOPIC

You probably learned about sexuality in a rather awkward and haphazard manner. Kids who are twelve or thirteen sometimes receive their total sex education from parents when they come in from school and find a sex book on their bed. Other parents take their children to a physician for a five-minute discussion about the whole matter. These approaches aren't the most supportive, are they? In fact, what is seen, sensed, and inferred is often the greater influence.

Thinking about your own childhood, you probably wished for more honest sexual communication. And your parents probably wanted to give you more detailed information and discussions. Instead, they either didn't, or they did it badly.

Much of the child's early learning experiences about sexuality relate to negative messages or nonverbal cues. Some of the child's first sexual experiences are touching the body and feeling smooth, soft, warm, and sensuous skin. These tactile experiences may be interrupted when parents notice the child playing with those "private parts," as the genital area is sometimes called. Parents may become embarrassed or angry. This response is one of the first messages a child has about his or her body. It often says that there is something forbidden or bad about "that" part of oneself.

As the infant grows into childhood, a natural curiosity develops about the same sex as well as of the opposite sex. Unfortunately for us, children don't phrase their questions or curiosities in the nice, polite, philosophical, or ethical innuendoes that we have learned. Instead, children walk up and bluntly ask beautifully innocent questions that leave even the most competent adult groping for words. For example, how would you respond to this simple, direct question posed by a five-year-old? "Daddy, how come Adam got to see naked women, and you won't let me look at naked women's books?"

Parents generally take pride when children inquire about the world around them. Questions of a sexual nature, however, seem to provoke quite a different reaction. When little Billy walks over to Aunt Jane, who is eight months pregnant, and says, "How is your baby gonna get out?" neither mother nor dad is pleased as punch that questions are signs of an intelligent mind. Instead, they scold him for being such a bad boy. "How do you think Aunt Jane felt?" they demand.

Initial anxieties about who we are as male or female often relate to a parent's awkward or negative reaction. You weren't born anxious—you learned to be. And learning to reshape these early anxieties can be difficult because sexual communication throughout your life continues in indirect and hidden messages. A residue of the awkward topic continues to influence you.

PARENTAL AVOIDANCE

Many parents hope that ignoring a child's sexuality means that they will not have to deal with it. Sometimes this works. They aren't, however, facing the consequences of their actions. Avoidance of direct conversation opens the possibility for misinformation and/or guilt, either about the simple and natural pleasures of touching the body or about the complex interactions between the sexes. Pleasures experienced by the child can become interwoven with guilt and negativism.

Parents would feel better if children pretended to be sexless little human beings. Of course, the parent was not able to ignore his or her own feelings, but it would greatly ease his or her anxieties if children became sexual only after leaving home!

Parents often encourage their children to be sexually backward or ignorant. They hope that it's better that the child is sexually ignorant than it is to reveal themselves as uninformed. Often, the most dreaded aspect of child raising is dealing with sexuality. If we reverse the wornout joke that has the child ask a parent, "Where did I come from?" most parents would say "Chicago" rather than try to respond to the sexual facts of life.

Put off, avoid, and ignore if you will. Yet children make inferences about their bodies and the reproductive processes very early. This suggests that they are often ready for the answers to sex questions between the ages of three and six. Rather surprising, then, that many parents finally scrounge up the courage to have that initial sex talk when the child is thirteen.

When children are left ignorant about basic body processes, they conjure up fears and misconceptions. Further, today's children are continually exposed to so many contrasting ideas about sexuality through the various media that a parent who remains silent can expect the child to draw together a potpourri of information and misinformation.

Some parents intentionally provide misinformation. For example, daughters are frequently told that kissing or petting can get them pregnant. This kind of scare tactic is designed to keep females out of trouble. Obviously, children eventually learn the truth. I have yet to talk to an adult who was glad a parent lied to him or her about some aspect of sexual information. As a parent, realize that avoidance, whether in the form of putting-off or half-truth answers does not provide the support and positive regard that builds better lines of communication.

LECTURE OR DISCUSSIONS?

Do you lecture to your child? When most parents decide to tell their child about sexual matters, the conversation is exactly that—telling them. They sit the child down and tell him or her sensitive warnings, such as "Keep your pants zipped" or "Don't put out before marriage." These comments aren't likely to stimulate a dialogue. If this is your manner, the question, "Is there anything else you want to know?" determines its own answer.

Parents may use such abrupt conversations for safety. To discuss is to risk answering additional questions. Fearing a dialogue, parents often set up the communication as a one-sided, easily controllable monologue. Having told the child what not to do, the parent can breathe a sigh of relief that the task is done.

These monologues are rarely followed by later, positive conversations. Parents may want to examine the likely effects of negative lectures. Such lectures tend to scare children, but they don't explain much. Negative messages about masturbation, for example, don't stop the act; they simply create a conflict in the child. More than likely, parents in the past couldn't discuss masturbation in other than negative terms because that was the extent of their information. Many sexual monologues by parents may be presented for the same reasons: They don't know the whys. Sexual discussions with your children can help you to better understand your own values. It may require a little reading on your part, but it is worth the time, both for you and your child.

Efforts to bring sexual understanding and acceptance makes a difference in the child's self-perception and in his or her perception of others. Recognize, too, that the more clearly the child understands your own sexual attitudes and values, the more likely he or she is to accept those values.

WHY PARENTS FAIL

Why, in the midst of this supposedly enlightened age, don't parents talk more to their children about sexuality? We've already seen some of their basic fears about approaching the subject. Yet there are other reasons that may help you move toward more positive dialogues.

Parents are inhibited by the appearances that suggest a really swinging, uninhibited sexual age. Looks can be deceiving, however. You may realize that media presentations of sexuality have not created a magic elixir to provide yourself and others the gift of verbal comfortableness. Discussions in magazines, for instance, have not yet reversed long-standing concepts and teachings that sexual matters were not to be openly talked about. Today's parents are barely more than four or five generations from their Victorian heritage.

And certainly, if today's youth believe that they have received inadequate information from parents, it seems clear that their parents did not fare any better. Sexual ideas formed over many years aren't likely to change overnight.

There is nothing inherent about participation in the coital

act that wipes away misinformation collected over a period of years. Nor does participation in the coital act automatically eliminate verbal awkwardness, discomfort, or language inadequacies. Bits and pieces of sex education learned by parents during developmental years continue to be incomplete or inaccurate. Many parents believe and teach, for example, that the urinary and vaginal openings are the same, that females shouldn't wash their hair during menstruation, or that males shouldn't have coitus the night before participating in sports activities. These ideas are often passed along to children.

Parents' sexual language is not always a comfortable language. Basically, there are only two languages in which to describe coital activity and body processes: street language and technical-medical terms. Although parents may enjoy using street language in the company of friends, those same words seem inappropriate in discussions with their children. As for medical terms, many parents can't pronounce the words or discuss them without awkwardness. Then, too, many people aren't sure what the words actually mean.

Parents often fear that their children know more about sexual matters than they do. The feeling seems to be that although the new wave of sexual awareness has passed by the parent generation, children are far more enlightened.

Parents feel a double bind. You may want and wish to discuss sexual matters with your children. Perhaps you haven't learned to be comfortable in doing so, and the risk of being foolish to your children is too threatening. But wishing that you possess a certain ability to talk about sex does not magically provide you with the skill.

There is also the attitude that frank and honest conversations on issues such as birth control and male-female relationships are synonymous with giving permission to engage in coital activities. Contained in this attitude is the belief that introduction to sexual information raises the sexual curiosity in children and thereby encourages sexual activity. In reality, the reverse is more likely to be true.

Parents see sexual discussions as the opening of Pandora's box of troubles. The fears, anxieties, and doubts between parent and child are often an apparent but unspoken concern in the relationship. A mother recently told me that she would be terribly upset to know that her college-age daughter was having sexual relations with her steady boyfriend. Yet she hadn't discussed this with her daughter. In a brief talk with the mother, it was clear that her major fear was pregnancy. I encouraged her to talk with the young woman and share her concern. I suggested that she convey her recognition of the daughter as an adult who is capable of making wise decisions. The conversation should also include her concerns that the young woman have a chance to express her talents and education before taking on the responsibilities of a family. This honest dialogue, during which she demonstrated that she trusted her daughter's abilities and yet which exposed her own fears, opened the way for what turned out to be a beautiful and sensitive discussion between the two.

Parents are often surprised that when they make an effort to discuss and show a willingness to listen, children seem more responsible and responsive than the parents had assumed them to be. Such discussions tend to create more respect between the parent and child.

A major reason why parents fail as sexual information sources for children is best described by one basic emotion: vulnerability. That feeling begins with the parents' own lack of formal sexual education and continues in their inability to convey information to children.

But the feelings of vulnerability can be overcome. First, you need to recognize and accept the reality of that emotion. And second, you need to take the risk and cast aside your fear by communicating sexual information to the child. Practice makes perfect. You'll be surprised how much easier it gets after the initial plunge.

Another reason that parents fail is because they fear the child's sexuality. Both parents and children are, in fantasy and reality, aware of the other's sexuality. They simply choose not to bring it to the surface. I know a father who is preparing to teach sexual seminars, yet he has never talked to his own seventeen- or twenty-four-year-old daughters about sex. I inquired whether his wife has talked to their daughters. He assumes that she has, but he doesn't know. It may be that he is not quite ready to identify the sexuality of his own daughters if he doesn't have to. Often, it is the same emotion of denial that children have when they are faced with the possibility that their parents have sexual feelings.

Many parents fail because they see sex education as being limited to the boundaries of gender. Mothers should talk to daughters, whereas fathers should talk to sons. Why? The input and support derived from a member of the opposite sex can be equally as helpful as information from the same sex—perhaps even more so.

In essence, parents fail because they don't talk to their children.

AVOIDING A COMMUNICATION GAP

Parents who provide a comfortable setting for sexual discussions can bridge the generation gap that exists between parent and child. Meaningful conversations are especially lacking in early adolescence, when the child experiences new and bewildering body changes. During that period, different messages surface about the opposite sex and about how to deal with changing relationships. Previous stereotypes, such as "little boys are bullies" or "little girls are sissies," are replaced by male and female coital desires. Unfortunately, parents don't explain or reduce the arising sexual anxieties and misinformation. Children go through these years with the information provided by the bravado discussions and natural curiosity of peers and the sexual images set up by the media. The relationships between parents and their adolescents could be more positive if better sexual communication developed. This area of the parent–child relationship frequently continues to be one of distance and avoidance. Yet the adolescent is always learning from his or her parents. The question remains, is the information helpful or harmful?

From this exploration of parent–child communication, it becomes apparent that the child often does not receive an adequate or thorough discussion about sexual matters from parents. Rather, the developmental years are spent splicing together what is sensed, overheard, and communicated, often in negative concepts. Little positive or direct interaction occurs between parent and child that might alleviate the resulting fears, anxieties, misconceptions, or guilt feelings experienced in childhood and adolescence. Are you the parent who builds the child's positive self-image, or are you in the other category? You decide.

MASTERING THE IMPOSSIBLE

You can learn to talk to your children about sex. You are well on your way when you determine that you will be the major source of sexual information for your child and that you will provide good, sound sexual information.

Remember that parents often assume that they give more information than is actually given. When I speak to an audience of parents, I ask, "How many believe that you are the major source for teaching your children sexual information?" Most parents raise their hands. On the other side, when speaking to college students, I find that about one out of twenty feels that their parents are the major source.

I have included certain ideas that you may want to heed when talking to your child. Naturally, the most important consideration is simply that you make the effort.

1. *Start with preschoolers.* Don't make the mistake of waiting

until the child is an adolescent. Begin sometime before the child starts school.
2. *Keep it initially simple.* The first questions can usually be answered with one or two statements. Don't feel, when a question first comes up, that you must immediately sit down and describe the entire process. For instance, if Susie asks why she doesn't have a penis like Johnny, you only have to say, "Because boys and girls are different. Johnny has a penis that is special for him and you have a vulva or clitoris that is special for you." If you provide simple, factual information, it is likely that the child will later ask for additional information.
3. *Invest in resource materials.* Many parents do not feel that they can adequately explain body processes or reproduction. It isn't necessary for you to become an authority or develop an encyclopedia of information. Instead, depend on other people's studies to explain these important facts clearly. Sex education for children is the one area of sexual writings that is generally well done. The styles range from cute books with cartoon drawings to more highly detailed treatments with photographs. Some titles follow.

Andry, **Andrew C.**, and **Schepp**, **Steven**. *How Babies Are Made.* New York: Time-Life Books, 1968. (Cartoons accompanied by a conservatively written text.)

Fleishhauver-Helga. *Show Me.* New York: St. Martin's Press, 1975. (Photographs and an explicit text.)

Gordon, Sol, and **Gordon, Judith.** "How Babies Grow." *Ms.* 9 (March 1976): 75–78. (My choice: a brief but thorough three-page article that is clear, honest, and beautifully written.)

These are only three of the many. A local book store probably has several to choose from. Select one that fits your own attitudes. Sit down with your child and read the book aloud. Afterwards you will be able to answer questions that may have stimulated the child's curiosity. You can probably manage one or two questions, even though the thought of handling the entire process was overly intimidating.

You may also want to explore sexual information books of a broader nature. I recommend these general sex education sources:

Demarest, Robert and **Sciarra, John**. *Conception, Birth and Contraception.* New York: McGraw-Hill, 1969.

Gordon, Sol. *Parenting.* New York: Oxford Books, 1975.

Hettlinger, Richard. *Growing Up with Sex.* New York: Seabury Press, 1971.

Hunt, Morton. *Sexual Behavior in the 1970s.* Chicago: Playboy Press, 1974.

Katchadourian, Herant, and **Lunde, Donald.** *Fundamentals of Human Sexuality.* New York: Holt, Rinehart, & Winston, 1972.

Kelly, Gary F. *Learning About Sex: The Contemporary Guide for Young Adults.* Woodbury, N.Y.: Barron's Educational Series, 1976.

Leokum, Arkady. *Tell Me Why—Answers to Questions Children Ask About Love, Sex, and Babies.* New York: Grossett & Dunlap, 1974.

McCary, James Leslie. *Sexual Myths and Fallacies.* New York: Van Nostrand Reinhold, 1971.

4. *Be honest.* Don't resort to fairy tales just because you feel uncomfortable responding to a question. Always give honest information. Never say anything that the child will later learn is incorrect. If your child can trust you to be

truthful, another positive aspect is added to the general parent–child interactions.

5. *When you don't know.* One mistake that parents frequently make is an unwillingness to say, "I don't know." Although you have been honest and helpful with the sexual information, there may come a time when you don't have all the answers—who does? Don't panic. Don't see this as a tragedy. Be honest with your child and simply say, "I don't know. Why don't we both do some research and see if we can find the answer. I would like to know that, too." For you and your child, sharing a learning experience can create a bond. It identifies you as a very human person.

6. *What to do about embarrassment.* At times, expect to feel embarrassed, awkward, or inadequate. Everybody does. The important idea is to charge ahead anyway. Depending on your personality, you may even want to share your feelings with your child. You may confide that because nobody talked openly with you about sex, you sometimes feel uncomfortable talking about sex. That, however, is why you are discussing sexual matters—because you want him or her to feel at ease with sexuality.

7. *Keep it in discussions—not lectures.* Many parents feel their children don't want to learn about sexuality from their parents. All too often that situation can be traced to the parents' conversational approach: lecture instead of discussions. Nobody likes to be lectured to. And when parents lecture children, opportunities for asking questions or exploring values are eliminated. If you are unwilling to listen to your child's concerns about the emotional aspects of sexuality, you may be forcing him or her to give greater acceptance to the values of peers. Discussions allow the child to raise questions, to consider possibilities, and to wonder why things are as they are. Discussions are also times when you can present the reasons why you have chosen your particular sexual values and attitudes. If

children adequately understand your position, they are more likely to incorporate those values as their own.
8. *Use correct vocabulary.* If you aren't comfortable with sexual terms—learn to be. Make sure that you pronounce the words correctly and that you practice simple definitions of the terms. As you work to become familiar with the terms, you will also find yourself feeling more comfortable in discussions with your child.
9. *Consider it an ongoing process.* See the sex talks between you and your child not as a one-time event but rather as an ongoing process. That process begins with the basic body processes for your preschooler and continues through the more complex interactional aspects of the male-female sexual relationships for teen-agers. That effort can establish another dimension in the relationship between parent and teen-ager that provides greater understanding and respect.

SELECTED REFERENCES

Brenton, Myron. *Sex Talk.* Greenwich, Conn.: Fawcett Books, 1972.

Coombs, Robert H. "Inhibition in Verbal Sexual Communication." *Medical Aspects of Human Sexuality* 5 (April 1971): 152–163.

Freeman, Harvey R. "The Generation Gap: Attitudes of Students and of Their Parents." *Journal of Counseling Psychology* 19 (September 1972): 441–447.

Gadpaille, Warren J. "Counseling Parents with Sexually Active Young Teenagers." *Medical Aspects of Human Sexuality* 8 (July 1974): 127–128.

Gerson, Allan. "Promiscuity as a Function of the Mother–

Daughter Relationship." *Psychological Reports* 38 (February 1976): 113-114.

Hunt, Morton. *Sexual Behavior in the 1970s.* Chicago: Playboy Press, 1974.

Lewis, Robert A. "Parents and Peers: Socialization Agents in the Coital Behavior of Young Adults." *Journal of Sex Research* 9 (May 1973): 156-170.

Libby, Roger W., and **Nass, Gilbert D.** "Parental Views on Teenage Sexual Behavior." *Journal of Sex Research* 7 (August 1971): 226-236.

Lieberman, E. James et al. "How Much Should Parents Know About Their Teenage Children's Sexual Behavior?" *Medical Aspects of Human Sexuality* 13 (June 1979): 6-14.

Lopiccolo, Joseph. "Mothers and Daughters: Perceived and Real Differences in Sexual Values." *Journal of Sex Research* 9 (May 1973): 171-177.

Moore, James E., and **Kendall, Diane G.** "Children's Concepts of Reproduction." *Journal of Sex Education* 7 (February 1971): 42-61.

Moulton, Ruth et al. "Sexual Responsiveness in Women." *Medical Aspects of Human Sexuality* 4 (January 1970): 53-65.

Offer, Daniel. "Sexual Behavior of a Group of Normal Adolescents." *Medical Aspects of Human Sexuality* 5 (September 1971): 40-49.

Shipman, Gordan. "Sex Education Between Parent and Child." *Medical Aspects of Human Sexuality* 5 (May 1971): 114-128.

Sorensen, Robert C. *Adolescent Sexuality in Contemporary America: Personal Values and Sexual Behavior, Ages 13-19.* New York: Collins Publishers, 1973.

Suneri, A. J.; Sunder, J. H.; and Joicha, D. "Initial Sources of Sex Information: Percentage and Rank Order." *College Student Journal* 7 (November 1973): 20–23.

Thornburg, Hershel D. "A Comparative Study of Sex Information Sources." *Journal of School Health* 42 (February 1972): 88–91.

———. "Educating the Preadolescent About Sex." *Family Coordinator* 23 (January 1974): 35–39.

chapter 7
PEER SEXPRESSIONS

You grew up with a secret service, a CIA of sexual information. An underground network. Want to know something about sex? Then ask your peers. They'll gladly elaborate. The information may be right or wrong, adequate or inadequate, or sensible or insensible, but simply ask and you'll be told. The telling of the tale via the peer grapevine may be for better or worse. As a child, your friends told you and taught you about sex. As an adult, they continue to do so.

More than parents, your sexual partner, or any other face-to-face source, same-sex peers become the lifeline for sexual information. Consider the influence. In childhood, adolescence, and adulthood, your peers contribute sexual information, sexual acceptance, and sexual role models. You learn to imitate them and to find acceptance through similar attitudes and behaviors. Later on, you may even find it easier to talk to peers than to your partner about coital needs, wants, or problems.

How much, then, do you know about the interactions with these very important people? Are your communications with them basically supportive and positive, or are they troublesome? In order to stimulate awareness about your sexual communication with peers, answer these true-false statements.

1. I talk more to my peer group of the same sex about coital matters than I do with my coital partners. TRUE ___ FALSE ___
2. When talking to my peers, I frequently discuss my coital experiences. TRUE ___ FALSE ___
3. I exaggerate my coital experiences to peers. TRUE ___ FALSE ___
4. I am dishonest about my coital experiences with peers. TRUE ___ FALSE ___
5. I am often reluctant to express my opinions and attitudes. TRUE ___ FALSE ___
6. I use the manipulation tactics described by my same-sex peers to turn on my girl friend, boy friend, or lover sexually. TRUE ___ FALSE ___
7. My discussions about sexuality tend to be set in put-down statements about the opposite sex. TRUE ___ FALSE ___

Don't be concerned if you have a mixture of true and false responses. Answering one or two of the statements as true doesn't suggest problems. For example, at times it is appropriate and wise to be cautious about what you say. And on occasions, you may put down the opposite sex, especially when you think about someone who "did you wrong."

If, however, a majority of the items were marked true, peers may hinder more than help. These discussions with same-sex peers may encourage myths and fallacies and inhibit honest communication with the opposite sex. As a result, you may rely too much on peers, use poorly informed peer discussions to solve sexual problems or questions, or complain or boast to peers rather than talk openly with your coital partner.

Insights about peer communication among children, adolescents, and adults reveal an important part of you. Peer talk about sex provides a necessary outlet—fun and frolic or sensitive and serious. It helps us to laugh at ourselves and to love ourselves.

The openness of peer communication has a definite influence on sexuality. Look at peer communication, and you may better understand your own sexuality.

CHILDHOOD DISCUSSIONS:
"THE BLIND LEADING THE BLIND"

Remember your earliest childhood discussions about sex? Friends pass along details, much as they do in the old game of Gossip. The statement whispered from one person to another quickly bears little resemblance to the initial idea. So it goes with the childhood messages scattered around about sex: communicative pandemonium. Catch as catch can. Confused but willing half-pint comrades relate any and all information that filters down to them through older siblings, friends, and overheard adult messages.

Picture the difference between adult and peer talk. Even though adults were downright stingy, negative, hostile, or angry about revealing treasured sexual information, you could rely on peers to divvy up tantalizing ideas. The catch, as you now know, was the many missing or wrong bits of information. For example, young boys often pass around information that the female's opening is in front to easily accommodate the penis.

Sometimes children employ more than the spoken word. Much to the displeasure of parents and teachers, peers played giggly games of show and tell: Show-Me-Yours-And-I'll-Show-You Mine, Let-Me-Touch-Yours-And-I'll-Let-You-Touch-Mine, and You-Tell-Me-What-You-Know-And-I'll-Tell-You-What-I-Know.

Overall, childhood conversations were abundant, but they were not always accurate. The accurate details are sometimes the least likely to be accepted as truth. As an adult, you may find humor in your own surprise, confusion, and disbelief that people really did such funny things or that babies came about through such strange possibilities.

At best, sexual information about this puzzling process was disorganized and scanty: a hodgepodge of data pieced together by guess. But did you stop to question where your informed friends gained their facts? No. The concern about accuracy was overridden by the need to fill gaps in the bigger picture. A free handout is accepted for what it is. Take what you can get.

All too frequently, these patchwork discussions result in fears, misunderstandings, or inadequacies that remain in adulthood. Original concerns about how babies are made give way to more sensitive issues regarding attitudes and behaviors about the lovemaking or baby-making process. As the information then turns to the finer points of anatomy, myths and fables move from basic "hows" to more abstract questions of why and what.

Such basic questions as how and where "it" goes in are answered through contact with the opposite sex. Less obvious information never gets corrected.

Early images of a magic phallus or an insatiable (or insensitive) vagina are often supplemented by later peer talks. As adults, we bed down with these same childhood images of each other. They can get in the way. They can be an invisible wall between coital partners—scary images that we have not dealt with.

ADOLESCENT COMMUNICATION: PRESSURE TO CONFORM

Remember how important it was to belong, to be accepted as a member of "the" group when you were a teen—the desire to be a real prince or princess among peers? Whether the image was permissive or restrictive, you wanted to belong. A friend of mine tells about the summer she moved from the east side to the central junior high eighth grade. When a popular ninth-grade guy tried to grab a kiss, she replied, "I'm not sure whether nice girls at Central do that on a first date." Although she now laughs about the frivolous incident, her memories about the painful desire to do the right thing in order to belong were not so easily brushed aside. The issue in this innocent situation was not whether she wanted to kiss the young man or even whether she felt that kissing on a first date was appropriate. Rather, her anxious concern rested in a lack of knowledge about the defined acceptable behavior of the new same-sex peer group.

Another young woman getting ready for her first year in high school was taken out by a male upperclassman who flatly said, "Give in, or walk home. You might as well give in, because if you want to be popular, you'll be doing a lot of that." So she did.

Think back and discover the particular sexual pressures you felt from peers. Basically, your peers were the most available source of sexual information. This is especially true of same-sex peers. Equally important, your social position came from their acceptance.

As you remember those relationships, there may be a renewed awareness of that desire for sexual information as well as the need for acceptance—a struggle to win, place, and show all at the same time. These factors make conformity to perceived peer values a powerful force.

Realize, too, that because the adult community refuses to share sexual information, peer communication increases in importance. That adults knew the secrets of sexuality but refused to tell you or your friends must seem a paradox. Why would they know and not tell? What was too good or too bad to be told? Remember the mystery of mysteries and the frequent stumbling upon overt and covert clues that continually piqued your interest?

As a child, you didn't know that adults kept secrets because they were embarrassed or uncertain. Instead, you conjured all manner of fanciful possibilities concerning the reasons for secrecy. Children visualize adults holding the keys to the magic doors just a little beyond their fingertips.

A result of adult silence is that peers, through sexual discussions with each other, become highly regarded for their sexual openness. This regard creates a greater willingness to conform to the perceived sexual behaviors of peers. They become the high priests of information, lifting the sacred veils that separate you from the sexual truths.

Do you understand, then, the potential forces and powers exerted by peer sexual attitudes and behaviors? The telling of the tales and the sharing of the communicative ritual provide pressures that add to the influence of peers.

In addition to peer pressure, the adolescent years bring frustrating physical and emotional changes. Often those changes are experienced in a vacuum because little meaningful discussion transpires from adults or even peers. This time of transformation, combined with the hearsay about sexual behaviors, adds to the difficulties. Boasts of the magic phallus and its effects on Sleeping Beauty are all too thoroughly believed by the awkward, anxious youth.

Regardless of the uncertain feelings, the adolescent tries to maintain an expected image for friends—a mirror image. He or she wants to be as nearly like everyone else as possible.

Jamie recently joked with a friend, "I wish I could lose my virginity without having sex, because everyone knows I'm a virgin." Her comment reflects the attitude that these days everybody has sex. The fact that she doesn't engage in coitus makes Jamie feel different, somehow not a bona fide part of her friends' inner circle. She feels similar to someone with one blue eye and one green eye—different.

The common refrain heard by parents is, "But, Ma, everyone does, wears, or is . . ." Young people want to be like that special popular image, whatever it is: argyles, ponytail, crewcut, afro, straight jeans, flared jeans, fraternity hazings, marrying because of pregnancy, and getting or paying for the abortion. The "let me be me" cry actually translates to, "Please let me be like everyone else." Remember the earlier examples of the teen girls who made their decisions on the basis of popular demand? Popular is definitely believed to be better. A mirror image ensures acceptance.

Yet even though we want to belong, there is a tendency to reject the idea that we conform our behavior to that of others. "I'm not like everybody else, I'm different." We see others following the pack, but we don't think the same is true about ourselves. We tend to view ourselves as Thoreau did, as "marching to the beat of a different drummer." Isn't it interesting how we walk that line of being like everybody else, and yet we want to be different?

Because the physical and emotional changes combine with a recognition that social position comes from peer acceptance, sexuality has the dual faces of agony or ecstasy. Yet as adults, we tend to forget this. Because the memory fades, we often become insensitive to adolescent anxieties.

For the adolescent, the agony is real when he or she says, "I'll just die if he or she doesn't like me any more." But we hear young people and wax wise with pseudo-comfort statements, such as "Well, dear, it's only puppy love. You'll soon forget, and this will be something you'll laugh about later." Is it any wonder that kids don't want to talk to parents or adults? Perhaps kids have a point when they say, "Why should I tell you what is wrong? You wouldn't understand anyway!"

On the other hand, the ecstasy is the initiation into the other side of those feelings. They haven't yet become old hat or things accepted as habits. They are new, vital, and exciting—uncharted. They are also forbidden. There is the tendency to forge ahead to know it all and, at the same time, to fear the reality of the consequences.

At the same time that adolescents experience internal sexual feelings, same-sex peer talk creates certain leads to follow. The young adolescent must maintain his role through rituals of knowing more than he knows, doing more than he does, and having more than he has. With his male comrades, he must be able to tell the tallest tales with the best of them. Tall-tale skill becomes a good approach for his acceptance and approval. However, as he moves into later adolescence, the wisest is he who learns to say the least. A certain shrugging noncommittal expression signifies a world of sexual achievements that words could destroy.

In many cases, the adolescent leads his male friends to believe that far more is going on than actually happens. So how does this make the young man feel about himself? He must get out and out-Hertz Hertz. Number two tries harder. Also, guys know that lots of the bull sessions are exactly that—bull; but the image of the magic phallus must still be maintained.

If the young male fears that male peers might laugh at his sexual incapabilities, the anxiety is not lessened when he actually encounters the object of fear—the female. Dealing with her has a nasty two-edged blade of potential disaster to it. If the girls laugh, reject, make fun of, disdain, or ignore him, word also gets back to his male friends. Therefore, when approaching the female he is aware of the dilemma. His guard is up to protect himself.

Both males and females have their own particular egos to protect. Potential rejection is scary. And, powerful feelings of attraction contrast with feelings of repulsion. When you really think about it, unless the emotional and physical feelings of attraction were so intense, why on earth would anybody undergo such frightening situations? The potential rejection may explain one reason why adolescents talk in such negative terms about the opposite sex: They aren't repulsed by the opposite sex so much as they are repulsed by the possibility of rejection by that sex. Therefore, we protect ourselves through continual conversations with same-sex members—the group to protect us against The Group.

Males and females each develop ways to communicate

about the other. The major difference between male and female same-sex peer communication is that male communication is basically aggressive and active talk. As for the female, she talks to her friends in a more passive script. Whereas the male talks about making "the moves," the female talks about doing things to get his attention so that she can talk about what he tries or doesn't try and does or doesn't do. She rarely says that she lets him go as far as she actually does. She can't, because one of the main topics of conversation centers on those girls who will let boys do anything—those bad girls.

Some adolescent high-school girls hide more than they tell about their sexual experiences. They play out a ritual of amazement when they hear that another girl was reputed to have gone all the way. The feigned shock and disbelief must be convincing enough to demonstrate that, indeed, they would never permit themselves to be so indecently compromised or talked about. There is the pleasure of presenting oneself as worthy to judge such others as immoral because their own behavior remains pure and their virginities intact. Such comments include, "I never would have thought . . ." or "She certainly could have fooled me," or "I knew she was *that* kind of girl."

Yet females give other females permission to be sexual teases. In fact, there are times when females laugh together about getting guys as "hot and bothered" as possible and then act sweetly demure about actual penetration because they are "good" girls. They trade advice about techniques designed to really steam a guy up.

Their girl scout merit badge among other females depends on being able to tell the best story about coming the closest without allowing penetration. Marginal virginity, but technical virginity nevertheless. Is it any wonder that males have been confused about the female's sexual drive or needs?

These tactics received from other females don't encourage honest sexual communication between males and females. Rather, these discussions teach, in subtle ways, superiority to the male by reducing personal needs in favor of a certain power over the male. Can we doubt the potential for false coital communication between partners later on? Permission is granted to use coitus not as a sharing or giving act but rather as a means to increase self-esteem by dishonest communication with males.

It is difficult to change communicative patterns for which we have been applauded. Our initial learning of dishonest sexual communication between males and females is less easy to overcome than most people realize. And what can occur is that females interact through a phony dialogue about coitus without realizing what is taking place. They see that the other person is not responding to them as they would like, but they cannot decipher that their sexpressions have created or contributed to the discomfort between partners.

Similarly, when males use their coital activities as a means to gain masculine pride from other guys, they set in motion exploitative attitudes and behaviors toward females. It reinforces a masculine myth that says that it isn't manly to desire emotional closeness with women. This creates problems in the ways a male relates to his coital partners and to his daughters as well.

In later adolescence, females often find it easier to be more open to same-sex peers about their intimacies. They sometimes discuss the reasons why they do or don't have sex. Some reasons run counter to all the smooth persuasive tactics that males believe are successful. Among one group of college women, several agreed that sometimes it is simply easier to give in than to argue.

At the same time that more open conversations exist, another kind of female communication is increasing: It runs parallel to the peer communication of younger adolescent males. Extremely explicit, the colorful words and salty content often rival any male conversation for ribald intent and flavor. These young females tell all, detail by detail. In addition, these females talk about various aspects of their coital experiences in mixed groups, although perhaps the talk is not as descriptive as that of males. It seems to establish that they are not going to be left behind the times if the times suggest a more permissive sexuality. There's little research to indicate the conversational tone in later adult years, but we can assume that just as the young adolescent male often tones down his sexual discussions, so will this female tone down her "show and tell" talk.

Perhaps now you remember a little more clearly those years that we adults often describe as "the best years of our lives." They are good years to look back on because the agonizing embarrassments and frustrations now seem humorous when the facts of sex are just a part of everyday life rather than an incomplete riddle. We have forgotten the bad and remember only the good. Your children are right when they say that you don't understand; you may not remember the reality. Instead, through your children, you want to relive those years vicariously as you wanted them to be—not as they really were.

ADULTHOOD: THE LAND OF AGAIN

Adulthood. That's "where it's at." Kids can hardly wait to grow up and taste the privileges reserved for those over twenty-one. Adults are known to "do their own thing," answer to no one, say what they want to say, do what they want to do. There is no need to conform. You know everything that is known about sex. Right? Absolutely wrong!

Adulthood: the land of on your own, take care of yourself, don't need anybody else, totally self-supporting. But it's not quite that way, is it? We talk about adulthood as though it were an ending. Instead, it is another beginning. Adults still need support, love, and acceptance from others, just as they did in childhood and adolescence. In fact, adults sometimes do the same crazy things in order to get noticed by others. And because we want our peers to like us, because we continue to receive information and acceptance from these significant others, we interact through both prior and present patterns. Some are good; some are bad.

Three persons now live inside your head and body: the child, the adolescent, and the adult. The sexual communication shared between you and your peers for each of these developmental ages has become a part of you. At different times, the experiences of each age may be used in order to get sexual information, attention, or acceptance. Your past communication experiences with peers become a part of your current interactions. Let's look at some of the sexual communication patterns that adults use to talk to other adults.

The Strong and Silent Man's Man

"Well, shucks, it wasn't nothin', fellows." The rugged outdoors guy who doesn't tell the sex jokes; who doesn't boast about the sexual conquests, although somehow everybody finds out; who isn't thought of as a love-em and leave-em guy, although he does; and who doesn't run around rescuing damsels in distress, although everybody knows that he would. What he doesn't say says it all.

The Good Ole Boy

The good ole boys love to collect around each other. Most prominently found in the heartland of the South, you will nevertheless see and hear these rather raucous souls anywhere and everywhere. They appreciate sexual talk best among their own good ole boys, but they appear to fit in comfortably with all male groups. Sexual discussions are tempered with backslapping, four-letter words among ribald tales, "I remember the time that, . . ." tail-swapping tales, and "Would ya take a gander at that girl's . . ." The good ole boy goes to heaven when he goes to a convention.

The Playboy

The playboy is a toned down good ole boy who generally isn't as comfortable with his peers. He may tend to distrust male peers slightly. His major sexual communication with males tends to be more indirect than direct. Being seen with the most attractive women in the most attractive fashions says what he wants said. Image-conscious, he never goes out with anything less than remarkably stunning women. The indirect nature of his communication with other males is geared to strike envy in the hearts of even the most successful business males. In direct conversations, he can just be one of the guys, although his apparent flair demands that he maintain a slightly superior air.

Timid Tom

This male, although liked by other males, is often thought of in the following terms: "There, but for the grace of God, go I." When it comes to sexual discussions, he can't tell a joke or describe an incident with any color and pazazz. He turns red as a beet at the strangest times and because of the most inappropriate and insignificant things. Never the leader of sexual discussions, he is instead a follower who frequently wishes that he were different.

Little Mary Sunshine

Among her female peers, she is easily recognized by such phrases as, "I can't believe it," or "Oh, my God, she didn't," or "I don't understand how . . ." Wide-eyed and innocent, Mary drops everything to get in on a sexual discussion with friends. Although she never gives the slightest information about her own sexual experiences, she has an uncanny ability to retrieve sexual facts and figures from even the most resistant female friend. With bulldog tenacity, the sugary sweet Sherlock Holmes has the lowdown on everybody.

Mata Hari

This little lady will tell everything her female friends want to know about the thrills, chills, and excitements—in the most intimate details. She's accepted by her group as the avant garde member of the group—always a step beyond; always aware of a new sexual word, position, remedy. Bold yet distant summarizes the character of her interactions. She tells so much so often that her peer group doubts her realm of possibility.

Susie Sorority

Susie is Miss Popularity. Her female peers hang on every word in an attempt to figure out what Susie has that they don't. When Susie says she does—they do. What Susie says she doesn't do—they don't do. She is the sexual model. It works for her; it will, perhaps, work for them. Her communication isn't one of vivid details because she isn't talking for attention—she already has attention. She is the princess telling her fans the sexual principles, answering their questions, and giving advice.

The Anti-Male Crusader

How to live with and without males is the basic theme of this female. Characterized by the descriptions of a multitude of male injustices and tragic flaws, these conversations tend to bemoan her fate in "woe is me because of him" prose. Both feminists and antifeminists assume this communication role. Although the content of the discussions varies because of the differing life styles of those who are or aren't feminists, the realities of the unhappiness brought about as a result of the male become the message.

The roles we take on to communicate about sex with our peers serve a purpose. They help us to get attention, acceptance, and information. Sometimes you feel like talking a bit like Mata Hari or the Good Ole Boy. It's fun and you enjoy it. Fine. There's nothing wrong with a change in moods. Too many of us, however, want to be crowd pleasers when it comes to sex talk—not just once in a while, not just for fun. Rather, we often take on sexual communication roles that hide our inadequacies.

The problem is that, as adults, we become entrenched creatures of habit. We get a circle of friends, and we stay with them. We talk the way they talk. We act the way they act. They may have negative ideas and attitudes about sex and the opposite sex. They may be misinformed or ignorant about sex. But we are influenced by their sexual attitudes and behaviors, or we want to influence them by our attitudes and behaviors.

Particularly in light of the sexual information, acceptance, and role models that come from our same-sex peers, the effect on our adult behavior can be powerful. Throughout childhood and adolescence, our same-sex peers suggest that the opposite sex are aliens. "Don't be totally honest, and don't let down your guard with them." We are led to believe that possession of a penis or a vagina respectively makes the owner speak with a forked tongue. As ridiculous as the idea is, have you entirely cleared away its absurdity? It is fear that creates suspicions about the people attached to the penis or the vagina.

We often live with the opposite sex, yet we still rely to a great extent on the sexual information of same-sex members in order to define our partners. Why not ask members of the opposite sex about their feelings, attitudes, and expectations? You might be surprised at how pleased they are that you care enough to ask. And you might also be pleasantly surprised at how very similar their needs are to your own.

One example of this is seen in adult males who will be more honest in sexual discussions with females than in those with other males. They feel less likely to be judged by females. They tell me that females have more sensitivity about listening to their sexual concerns in an honest manner. They don't compete with the female; they compete with other males.

In sexual workshops and seminars, I often have the males sit in an inner circle to discuss females while the females sit in an outer circle and listen. The communication situation is then reversed so that the females then talk about the males. It's an interesting little exercise. Although there is some bravado talk, members of the opposite sex are usually surprised to learn that the needs and wants of both sexes are so similar. Isn't it amazing that, although we spend so much time in relationships with the opposite sex, we spend so little time asking or telling them directly what we want and need?

DEVELOPING CONSTRUCTIVE PEER COMMUNICATION

Can you now identify certain roles that you take on when you have sexual discussions with peers? How do you participate in peer discussions about sex? Are you basically a follower or a leader? Are you constant, or do you change like a chameleon according to the mood or group in which you are involved? As you think about these and other questions, you can begin to develop more constructive peer communication. First go back to the initial seven questions you answered in the first part of this chapter (page 130). Write out each statement that you answered as true. At the end of that statement, write the word "because." For example, "My discussions about sexuality tend to be set in put-down statements about the opposite sex because . . ." Don't push for thoughts. Just let your mind begin to respond to the question. You will find that if you begin writing, the ideas will flow. Don't think or analyze—just write. You will be surprised at how much you can write if you don't censor your thoughts or concern yourself with grammar. This isn't an English essay. When you find that the flow of ideas has subsided, then read what you have written. This free flow of thoughts will probably reveal some rather interesting ideas about your attitudes. These insights will provide additional clues into your communicative behavior and needs.

Also, encourage yourself to gain awareness and insights from discussions with some of your friends who are opposite-sex peers. This will be difficult for some of you because many adults in this society don't maintain friends of the opposite sex. There is a popular notion that adult males and females can't be friends without being lovers. How unfortunate this antiquated idea is: It denies us the pleasure of knowing about fifty percent of the population—and there are some mighty fine people out there.

Finally, you are an adult now. It is no longer necessary for you to live by the patchwork of sexual ideas that you accepted as a child or as an adolescent. Take the time and effort to think out sexual ideas for yourself. Evaluate the ideas of your peers. Your decisions about sexual information are important, wouldn't you say so?

SELECTED REFERENCES

Balswick, Jack O., and Peek, Charles W. "The Inexpressive Male: A Tragedy of American Society." *Family Coordinator* 20 (October 1971): 363–368.

Bear, Sheryl; Berger, Michael; and Wright, Larry. "Even Cowboys Sing the Blues: Difficulties Experienced by Men Trying to Adopt Nontraditional Sex Roles and How Clinicians Can Be Helpful to Them." *Sex Roles: A Journal of Research* 5 (April 1979): 191–198.

Bednarik, Karl. *The Male in Crisis.* Trans. by Helen Sebba. New York: Knopf, 1970.

Cameron, Paul. "The Generation Gap: Beliefs About Sexuality and Self-Reported Sexuality." *Developmental Psychology* 3 (September 1970): 272.

Chapmen, Anthony J., and Gadfield, Nicholas J. "Is Sexual Humor Sexist?" *Journal of Communication* 26 (Summer 1976): 141–153.

Driscoll, Richard H., and Davis, Keith E. "Sexual Restraints: A Comparison of Perceived and Self-Reported Reasons for College Students." *Journal of Sex Research* 7 (November 1971): 253–262.

Fasteau, Marc Feigen. *The Male Machine.* New York: McGraw-Hill, 1974.

Gadpaille, Warren J. "Father's Role in Sex Education of His Son." *Sexual Behavior* 1 (April 1971): 3–10.

Harrison, James. "Warning: The Male Sex Role May Be Dangerous to Your Health." *Journal of Social Issues* 34 (1978): 65–87.

Hettlinger, Richard. *Sex Isn't That Simple: The New Sexuality on Campus.* New York: Seabury Press, 1974.

Hofmann, Adele D. "Adolescent Promiscuity." *Medical Aspects of Human Sexuality* 8 (May 1974): 63–64.

Hopkins, J. Roy. "Sexual Behavior in Adolescence." *Journal of Social Issues* 33 (1977): 67–85.

Kantner, John F., and Zelnik, Melvin. "Sexual Experience of

Young Unmarried Women in the United States." *Family Planning Perspectives* 4 (October 1972): 9-18.

Light, Harriet K. "Attitudes of Rural and Urban Adolescent Girls Toward Selected Concepts." *Family Coordinator* 19 (July 1970): 225-227.

MacCorquodale, Patrica, and **DeLamater, John.** "Self-Image and Premarital Sexuality." *Journal of Marriage and the Family* 41 (May 1979): 327-339.

Miller, Derek. "The Treatment of Adolescent Sexual Disturbances." *International Journal of Child Psychotherapy* 2 (January 1973): 93-126.

Mitchell, John J. "Some Psychological Dimensions of Adolescent Sexuality." *Adolescence* 7 (Winter 1972): 447-458.

Oakley, Ann. *Sex, Gender, and Society.* New York: Harper & Row, Pub., 1972.

Offer, Daniel. "Sexual Behavior of a Group of Normal Adolescents." *Medical Aspects of Human Sexuality* 5 (September 1971): 40-49.

Sorensen, Robert C. *Adolescent Sexuality in Contemporary America: Personal Values and Sexual Behavior, Ages 13-19.* New York: Collins Publishers, 1973.

Suneri, A. J.; Sunder, J. H.; and **Joicha, D.** "Initial Sources of Sex Information: Percentage and Rank Order." *College Student Journal* 7 (November 1973): 20-23.

Thornburg, Hershel D. "Ages and First Sources of Sex Information as Reported by Eighty-eight College Women." *Journal of School Health* 40 (March 1970): 156-158.

Wagner, Nathaniel; Fujita, Byron N.; and **Pion, Ronald.** "Sexual Behavior in High School: Data on a Small Sample." *Journal of Sex Research* 9 (May 1973): 150-155.

chapter 8
MEDIA
SEXPRESSIONS

Just as a mirror reflects an image of you, the media reflects an image of your sexuality. Isn't the media a reflection of society's sexual attitudes and behaviors? Or does the media become the "individual," and do you reflect the images represented by the media? Which do you believe is more correct? The answer is vital, because your sexuality is intricately bound and aligned to the media's presentation of sexuality. It is a dependent relationship. The media is a more willing and available source for sexual imagery and information than either parents or peers. A best friend. And such a friend—always there to provide support, answers, and personal acceptance. An advisor of sorts. That is what friends are for. And what do you supply in return? Respect, faithfulness, and, last but not least, the almighty dollar.

An almost perfect relationship. Give, ask, and get. Give (money), and you shall receive. Ask (for information), and you shall get. Why? Because sex sells. If you want to know about sex, the media will tickle your toes and other anatomical parts as well. It writes provocative, ribald, or even clinical sexual details. This builds circulation. It fills magazine pages with bare bodies and tempting titillations. This sells products. It splashes sex in books. This makes best sellers. All for you. An almost perfect relationship—almost.

There has been, as previously noted, a revolution—not a sexual revolution but a media revolution that infiltrates every aspect of sexuality. Why? Because there's money in sex, and that fact is exploited. In and of itself, that is neither good nor bad. It meets a need—your need and their need. What you must know is that some sexual ideas or images are more marketable than others.

A certain awareness of the media will help you to consider these basic questions wisely: What sexual attitudes do you currently hold as a result of information from media sources? How conscious are you about the possible effects of the media on your sexuality?

Your responses to these questions indicate your own education about its influence. Perhaps you answered by thinking that, although other people are clearly affected by the input of media, you are not. Are you sure? Do you know, for example, how extensive a source it is? Do you realize how its changing images change you? Are you aware that your hidden anxieties and frustrations benefit the media? Do you know that you accept without protest the sexual inaccuracies and misconceptions of the media?

You can learn to distinguish the good from the bad, the accurate from the inaccurate, the fantasy from the reality. In essence, you must separate the message from the media.

The following three sections barely scratch the surface, but they are an attempt to help you begin to evaluate the written media and its sexual influences. As you learn about media, keep in mind that you are what you think!

MAGAZINES

Casually pick up a magazine while waiting in a supermarket line or in the doctor's office. Do you look over your shoulder to see if anyone notices the topic of interest? The subject, in one form or another, is almost certainly sex. And it is unquestionably being presented in explicit terms.

Today, sexual topics include materials that would have made Don Juan blush or at least turn the page excitedly. Yet we read these selections in the most casual of attitudes and in the most traditional magazines. It's all there. What do you want to know? If you can name it, you can find it—and then some. The floodgates have been opened: Anything and everything goes. Over the past few years, there has been a tremendous increase in sexual materials.

So what, you say? Well, read on. Numbers of sex references aren't the only changes.

In addition to the increasing number of references, magazines have also altered their presentation of morality. Think about your own sexual standards and ideas. Have they changed any over the past ten years? Probably. If so, do you suppose that the media has changed your sexuality, or have your sexual interests and concerns changed the media? If there has been a shift in the media's presentation of sexuality, for whatever reason, it becomes a potential influence on the way you live.

Margaret Zube, for instance, conducted a study of the *Ladies Home Journal* from the years 1948 through 1969. The results demonstrate a departure from traditional sexual values. Notice this considerable difference in a relatively short period of time. The late 1940 writings presented a set system of moral standards. Traditional morality: This is right; this is wrong. The perspective, however, gradually changed in order to permit an individual the right to determine appropriate moral codes. Interesting? Well, here's the question for you again: Does this primarily reflect a change in the editorial staff, or does this reflect changes in your thinking?

This turnaround is not an isolated media phenomenon. One quick glance at the general content of women's magazines shows that current topics, as well as the approach to these topics, would not have been touched twenty-five years ago. Both monthly columns and article features assume open and honest discussions of sexuality: the orgasm; how to handle male impotence; sex on the college campus; swinging sex; incest; male and female infidelity; sexual problems of children; and, especially, how to become a better sexual partner. A few years ago, traditional women's magazines would not have spoken about these ideas, much less in such a nonjudgmental way.

At the same time that few subjects seem taboo, magazine editors puzzle over women and their feelings about male nudity. Can it be, they wonder, that the "sugar and spice" female peeks with voyeuristic pleasure at the male body? Surely not! Our moral code in years gone by declared that nice girls would scarcely be interested in such things. But I wonder why we are so unwilling in this day and age to consider the female's fascination or curiosity about frontal male nudity.

No one who has ever listened to a group of women talking about "that cute male tush," "those gorgeous thighs," or other assorted parts can doubt their interest in the total package—unwrapped. Women appreciate the male body, especially when they perceive that to do so is acceptable. Therefore, if there has been a lack of enthusiasm among females, it may relate to presentation rather than appreciation. For the most part, the photographs constitute a casual, in the buff, horsing-around-among-the-guys genre. You get the feeling that just beyond the camera his buddies are also washing the car, gathering wood, hopping on a motorcycle, or swimming in the surf. The implied relationship is more one of male camaraderie than one of male–female interacting. The bodies look terrific. But the total effect lacks the same flirtatious, provocative, seductive appeal that is used for female poses.

A little less extreme, but far more widely accepted, is the cute, coy, and flirtatious popularity of *Cosmopolitan*. The definite message declares that women are sexy, sensual creatures. Women are encouraged to be aggressive in their efforts to attract men, but at the same time, they are to appear soft and cuddly. For the sensuous woman, this approach speaks for more than permission to have and enjoy sex. Sensuality is presented as a way of life—at the least, a VIP—a Very Important Pastime. Its humor and upbeat tempo about sex is rather similar to that found in men's sexual magazines. Permission is most assuredly given for females to enjoy sex in a similar "sex is for fun" attitude.

How do you interpret these changes and approaches in women's magazines? Do you believe that these alterations in moral interpretations, the creation of sex as play, and the initiation of male frontal nudity have been instituted by us, the public, or by the media? Regardless of your answer, what has been the effect on American women and their relationships with men?

The greatest change in men's magazines came with the arrival of *Playboy* in 1953. Since that time, the provocative nude females have continued to tickle the fancy and fantasy of men. Basically, the only changes have argued whether or not there should be open beaver shots. Some say that the visible genitalia take away the seductive artistry and instead establish seductive pornography. Regardless of your opinion, they are formative images that shape your belief.

Basically, these magazines are seductive and sensuous. They cater to the Mr. Macho image; the James Bond manliness; the John Wayne cool; the Buck Rogers ability to conquer worlds, if not women. This image shows a man infinitely greater than the average guy—a superior sexual weapon. Terrific for fantasy. But, in real life, he may not always feel like being Mr. Macho/Bond/Wayne/Rogers. Yet who will tell him that it isn't continually necessary? Not his parents. Not his peers. Generally, not his lover. Fantasies are fun, but they don't always solve problems. Moreover, fantasies get confused with realities. Who can tell the young or older male that good sex doesn't require a female nymphomaniac or a nine-inch penis?

Consider, for example, this current problem. The penis wilts and hides and won't come out and play because the

New Woman, the Liberated Woman, scares him. Perhaps it isn't the New Woman who scares him as much as the writings about how intimidating the New Woman is. "The Sexual Demands of the New Woman"; "The Multi-orgasmic Female: What Male Can Keep Up With Her?" The new rhetoric makes her appear too demanding. If you listen to this, coitus seems to be a contest between partners. As indicated earlier, both males and females have been beautifully equipped by nature to enjoy the experience equally. Coitus is not a mutual competition; it is a mutual pleasure. Belief in such stereotypic images becomes dangerous. Males who read and accept the tales of the New Woman may find themselves participating in an unnecessary, but real, sexual crisis.

Generally speaking, however, men's sexual magazines stress a different approach to sexuality than do women's magazines. *Playboy*, for example, states under the title, "a magazine for entertainment." Their expressed purpose isn't to destroy sexual myths but rather to entertain with fantastic fantasy. *Playgirl* magazine also indicates under their title, "entertainment for women." Yet, in addition to nude photographs of the opposite sex and the erotic articles, contained within are articles about how to get him, how to win him back, or how to get over him. In fact, women's magazines, from *Redbook* to *Playgirl,* are filled with "how to deal with him emotionally" articles. Such a concept is rare among men's magazines, if you find it presented at all. Why? Well, this difference seems to derive from the societal attitude that woman is an accessory in a man's life. To woman, however, man is supposed to be her world. Therefore, she had best know all the "how to's." Man is to woman, by cultural definition, a statement about her completeness, her position in society, her social standing—a social standing that is not predicated on her own accomplishments. You'll find this attitude demonstrated in the oddest situations. During a recent Equal Rights Amendment meeting, the female speaker was introduced as Mrs. ___, whose husband's outstanding law career was described in detail before presenting her rather solid credentials. This seems to tell us that her relationship with him was more impressive than anything she might achieve on her own. Similarly, it seems a shame that women's magazines often encourage an attitude of getting him and keeping him as a means of achieving her self-worth.

MAGAZINE ADVERTISEMENTS

The world of advertising is a world of problem-solving, anxiety-reducing, pleasure-filling products and services—all for you, for your attention. And, not inconsequentially, for your money. These two are inseparable qualities, because without your attention, they would not get your money. Therefore, create a problem and construct a solution that reduces the anxiety, fills the pleasure, and meets the need. And how best to do that? Try using a sexual theme for the story line. Grab that attention by identifying or establishing a sexual need. Combine, for example, a basic need for food, shelter, clothing, or security with the equally basic, but more difficult to talk about, needs of sexual attraction, desire, stimulation, or satisfaction. Voilà—a consumer stampede. It works. We buy and aren't always aware of why we buy. Nevertheless, our concerns about sexuality provide a variety of selling approaches for the ad people. Notice, for instance, these typical sexual promises:

1. To make you more attractive.
2. To make you more sensual (an attitude or experience you may not feel is adequately conveyed to the opposite sex).
3. To make you good in bed.
4. To bring more members of the opposite sex into your life.
5. To take the humdrums out of your coital experiences. To create a new, rather than a boring, experience.
6. To make you irresistible—nobody is able to turn you down.
7. To turn timid souls into wild, free playmates.

8. To make you harder, softer, wilder, tamer, sexier, more innocent, sensitive, aggressive, and so on.

You weren't aware that you had so many sexual needs to be satisfied? Well, even if you don't know, it's the advertiser's job to convince you that you do. And what better way to sell a product than to promise to alleviate the sexual insecurities that aren't even shared with your closest friends? For a price range beginning at under a dollar for cosmetics, food, and health items to thousands of dollars for the right life-style image, naturally, we buy!

A creative approach to sexuality, wouldn't you say?—a complete story told through one picture and a few brief but well-phrased words. It creatively exhibits a strong influence on your life style and on your attitudes as well. The ad has to be strong in order to influence you and, thereby, achieve its goal. Even with a certain awareness, you may consider advertising the least consequential influence on your sexuality. Better think again. Billboards and magazines alone are substantial in number. But include, for a moment, television and radio ads. How many do you hear and see each day? Ten, twenty, or thirty? Guess again. Conservative estimates run as low as sixty per day, whereas the higher estimates go as high as five hundred. Sound rather incredible? Well, count the ads heard or seen in the course of one day. You'll be astounded at the total unless you never watch television, read a magazine, listen to the radio, or drive along the highway. The only means to avoid the messages is to become a hermit, because advertising is a natural part of your life—like orange juice and vitamins, gossip and the telephone, the flu and a headache. The ads and their impact: Images are there, and they do make an impact.

You can determine to be discriminating with respect to reading material and television, but how will you avoid advertisements? Actually, you don't want to avoid them. In many ways, they are an excellent source of information. You may wish, however, to identify the sexual agenda presented more clearly. Some ads are blatant; others are subtle. Some products are so blatant that they even shape their containers in the appearance of sexual organs. They stare at you from the store shelves or from the colorful magazine ads and dare you to resist their basic symbolism. Since many primitive tribes make images of the genitals and worship them, why should Madison Avenue pass up this bold approach? Why kid around? Instead, let it all hang out.

Other ads use double meaning words that may or may not refer to sexual parts or ideas. Upon looking at the total ad concept, there will be little doubt in your mind that such words are intended. What you see upon closer examination is deliberate. Far more ads than you imagine make promises of sexual security. Look for yourself—you'll see. Rare is the magazine that doesn't include ads designed to address some aspect of the sexual personality. It's a big influence, a prominent influence, and one that you will believe only by investigating for yourself.

In sexual communication courses or workshops, I generally touch on the use of advertising designed to soothe our feelings of sexual frustration or anxiousness. People enjoy learning to explore the simple written copy and photographs for sexual content. Nothing hidden, nothing subliminal, nothing a Ph.D. has to find—just messages that you aren't expecting. Once observed, however, it's easy to find the outrageously suggestive material.

In what magazines, you ask? In almost any.

To get you started in this revealing pursuit, let me describe a classic ad—a favorite of my audiences. Its intentions are direct and honest, which is more than can be said for many ads. It is openly sexual and quite charming, even if sexist in nature. This masterpiece of sexual subtlety describes coital activity from start to finish and was achieved by Subaru of America, Incorporated. Its pleasant black and white picture shows an attractive man and woman posed on a boat dock behind a Subaru GL Coupe. The large copy reads as follows: "The

Subaru GL Coupe. Like a spirited woman who yearns to be tamed." In the smaller, less obvious print is this fulfilling tale:

> The Subaru GL Coupe is waiting for you. Sleek. Agile. The sculptured lines of the one piece body invite you in. With front wheel drive she's different. A step ahead of the others. Go to her. Let her cradle you in the softness of her highback reclining bucket seats. Surround yourself with the lushness of her interior appointments. The GL Coupe is ready. Now. Turn her on. Lead her to the open road. This is where the Subaru GL Coupe wants to be. Unleash the relentless power of her 1400 cc quadrozontal engine. Control the Coupe's every movement—her every twist and turn—as you take hold of her rack and pinion steering. She'll make it smooth with her four wheel independent suspension. She'll carry you away as she peaks to the red line of her tach. The Subaru GL Coupe is yours. Waiting for you. And one more thing, she costs so little to keep happy.

Remove certain words, but do not take them out of context, and the paragraph becomes the description of an extremely pleasurable coital encounter:

> . . .The one piece body invites you in . . . she's different. A step ahead of the others. Go to her. Let her cradle you in the softness of her . . . seats. Surround yourself with the lushness of her interior appointments. . . . [she] is ready. Now. Turn her on. Lead her. . . . This is where . . . [she] wants to be. Unleash the power. . . . Control . . . every movement—her every twist and turn—as you take hold. . . . She'll make it smooth. . . . She'll carry you away as she peaks. . . . [She] is yours. Waiting for you. And one more thing, she costs so little to keep happy.

Few ads are so openly descriptive about their aim to make sexual successes part of your buying. The greater number that use sexuality aren't happily detailing the coital act. Rather, they promise to cure your sexual anxieties, frustrations, and fears, thereby leading to the coital act. Deodorants, liquors, cigarettes, clothing, beauty aids, and countless others: They all use our sexual weak spots in order to persuade. "It" makes you better, or "It" helps you "make out." Their purpose is not to comfort you but rather to make you uncomfortable enough to buy. Your concern must persuade you to plop down the hard cash for their product—not any other. They must, in one sense or another, offer more. In many cases, the "more" is greater sexual security elicited by exposing your greatest sexual insecurity.

Other advertisers select your sexual uncertainties as the target. Should I do this or that? Should my behavior be naughty or nice? Apparently, advertising people believe that the naughty but nice quandary sells, because they often repeat to women the mutual theme of innocence and sexiness. Look for yourself. You'll see this theme in a number of magazines. Advertisers seem aware that many American women aren't truly at ease about sex, nor are they innocent in a nineteenth-century fashion. Most of us are wandering somewhere beyond a Victorian naiveté, yet we are not solidly comfortable with the perceived sexual permissiveness. Therefore, the mutual theme of innocence and sexy has wisely been adopted—wild yet innocent, sensual but innocent, natural yet innocent. The ads say "yes" to things that your mother never would. For a few dollars, they grant permission. You buy that permission. Behave as you want, they suggest. It's all right. Be sexy but retain that aura of innocence for your conscience. Be sexy, yet still be a good girl—a bargain, indeed—at the price of just a few dollars.

Perfume ads are among the greatest users of blatant suggestions for allurement and passion. Members of the opposite sex are guaranteed to flock around and send you to the moon if you use one tiny dab of an erotic smelling agent. Jovan, Incorporated, for example, produces Musk Oil for both men and women. Their ads are built around sensual power and passion. Why buy a perfume that simply makes you smell good when Jovan fills two special needs? First, a splash brings the opposite sex to your side, and, second, it provides the most pleasant coital experiences. In addition to this imagery, Jovan includes an interesting little twist to the needs fulfillment of males and females. The ad for women says, ". . . Suddenly you're more female," whereas the male-oriented ad promises, ". . . It will probably put more life into your women." Another ad for Jovan simply states " . . . dedicated to the proposition."

Many sexual ads hint at helping you to become better in bed. Kayser-Roth Intimate Apparel Company, Incorporated, presents a rather novel theme for the woman who feels no problems about her coital abilities. The photograph shows an attractive woman wearing a long, flowing nightgown. Behind her stands a classically tall, handsome man. The written copy boldly asks, "Marvelous in bed? It's not enough any more." The idea behind it is that, at one time, being a good female partner did ensure success but now it takes more. Whatever "more" is, Kayser-Roth will take care of it for you.

The reason for this brief little stroll down the avenue of advertisers is, by now, I hope, apparent. The influence is greater than simply winning your pocketbook. In their efforts to win the heart strings that are attached to the purse strings, advertisements set up sexual images designed to ease sexual anxieties and discomforts. Through images seen again and again, through the jingles, through the cute phrases, through the erotic portrayals of the sensuous and sexual, we buy more than a product. We also buy permission for a life style linked to that product's image. Potentially, we become that image, and, as with any stereotype, if it is a good, healthy, beneficial image—great. On the other side, all too many stereotypes are narrow images made to fit someone else's needs—in this case, the company's needs.

In brief, advertising is an important element in our lives. It is a wise consumer, however, who knows not only the product but the advertising strategy as well. Sexuality in advertising isn't necessarily bad. Sometimes it's rather charming, humorous, and fun. Occasionally, it is even informative. But you need to be aware of the intended sexual image. That's only fair.

SEX MANUALS

By definition, manuals are designed to make things more simple with instructions or information about a subject or task. Hence, they deserve the label of "how to" books. You've probably read at least one: a "how-to-do-it" marriage or sex manual, as they are known. They read something like the following:

> ... Insert Part A into Part B when the male party has appropriately warmed the female party by the adequate degree of foreplay (See Section C, Fore Factors in Chapter Three, Before the Parts Shall Twain).

A bit facetious perhaps, but the message is clear. In many ways the "how-to-do-it" approaches confuse people and thus lead to an unintentional comedy of errors. Place this leg over that leg and that leg over this arm and that arm over the other leg (now wait a minute, isn't there an extra arm and leg in there some place?). The male partner does this; the female partner does that: Insert; now, thrust; and so on.

This type of minute detailing describes only one facet of the "how to's." Here are some other reasons why these books gain popularity. They teach or instruct coital factors in order to achieve the following:

1. Build confidence.
2. Correct misinformation.
3. Establish a sense of morality in that what you do is not something relegated to the animal kingdom.
4. Instruct in anatomy and physiology.
5. Instruct in general hygiene.

6. Provide a sense of what the other sex wants or likes.
7. Describe birth control methods.
8. Describe the mechanics of sex—that is, positions, timing, control, and so on.

The value of most "how to" sex books is dubious at best, because few present ideas without also presenting areas of misinformation. Reading many sex manuals is a matter of divvying up points—here's one for my side; here's one for your side. They aren't sensitive about the mutual needs of both partners. Unfortunately, too many of the authors follow the mistaken ideas of society in general. If you examine the coital myths and stereotypes in society closely, you'll find them often repeated in manuals.

These stereotyping problems can be more easily identified by examining these books. I'll present some basic areas in order to help you notice the flaws more readily. You can: It is not that difficult.

You need an awareness of certain of the problems found in "how to" books because they write about how he can/she can't or about how she won't/he can't. In many ways, they hinder people from learning more pleasurable and sensitive ways of interacting sexually. You need such books partly to allay curiosity and partly to correct any misinformation learned from direct sources, such as parents and peers. Unless the errors are blatantly obvious, you may accept the same misinformation in print that has become part of your relationship—for better or worse.

My review of several sex manuals supports the findings of earlier studies. Although some positive changes are being made in these readings, many leading manuals continue to confirm images of feminine passivity and masculine aggressiveness. That is to say, the accepted public social manners for males and females transfer to the private confines of the bedroom. Males are instructed in the finer points of arousing, pleasing, and satisfying her. The female orgasm has arrived! The title of one book, not necessarily a manual, reads, *Any Woman Can.* The emphasis on female orgasm in manuals seems more inclined to suggest that every woman should. It has become a responsibility to herself and to her partner—the badge of success. Exactly how her orgasm comes about is quite a different matter. Following the social images of female passivity and masculine aggressiveness, the male is supposed to be actively engaged toward their success. Why? Well, it appears that many of the manuals espouse the traditional but false beliefs:

1. Men have greater sexual drives; therefore, if the female is to find hers, he *must* help!
2. The female is orgasmically inferior to the male's ability to have and experience orgasm. Therefore, she needs his help. (This is a rather strange dichotomy in the manuals, as they also discuss the multi-orgasmic female.)
3. Coitus is not a mutual experience, both in responsibility and pleasures.

Couples may be confused about how they can bring about this misunderstood feminine phenomenon. Manuals rarely offer much sound advice. First of all, sex manuals describe the orgasm as something elusive, an ultimate experience that the couple aims toward. And, basically, as represented in manuals, she lies waiting for him to make it happen momentarily. How ridiculous. Doesn't she have a voice and a body to share both the responsibility and pleasure for their coital experience? Can't she tell him what she wants or likes? Apparently not, because sex manuals rarely describe the importance of talking about coitus, in bed or out. This misinformed attitude assumes that couples look at each other, touch each other, feel each other, and experience each other in such a way that each magically knows what the other wants and means. That is simply not true. In even the best relationships, people must talk in order to know the feelings of the other.

One of the biggest problems with information contained

in sex manuals is the idea of inequality between male and female activity. Again, following the traditional ideas of dating, males must initiate excitement and pleasure in females. She, again, is passive, whereas he must be excessively active. In order to be a good partner, he is required (by the implications in the manual instructions) to know exactly what she needs and wants—rather in the fashion of a guessing game, since manuals don't advise much about talking to one's partner effectively. Think about the absurdity. It is not very likely that one partner could achieve this ability, is it? Do you generally know what your partner wants or is thinking about during coitus? The answer is both yes and no. Sometimes you do; sometimes you think you do; sometimes you know that you don't know. Why make a guessing game out of sex? Why not be honest instead and simply tell him or her what you want—for your pleasure and for your partner's pleasure?

You'll also find another general fable of female relationships in sex manuals. When a relationship is fine, manuals stress that the male is doing a good job—giving a fine performance. This implies that if there are no problems in the coital experiences, he is a sexual gem—a superman. However, when a problem exists, writers of the manuals assume that it must stem from her problems. The approach works to answer, "What can be done to correct her problem?" How can manual writers know that it is her problem?

Why must he perform better than his partner? Why must we assume that any problems are automatically hers? When you read manuals with stereotyping, put them down. This imagery will not build the mutual and sensitive coital relationship that you desire. Every relationship is different, and the most important thing you can do to build a positive experience is to learn to express your coital wants and needs.

As I have been suggesting, sexual stereotypes can be hidden deterrents to good relationships between the sexes. It seems that our acceptance of stereotypes is no less troublesome to the readers and writers of sex and marriage manuals.

YOUR CONCLUSIONS

Well, how do you see the sexual images presented by the media? How do you answer the initial questions: Isn't the media a reflection of society's sexual attitudes and behaviors? And does the media become the "individual," and do you reflect the images represented by the media? Furthermore, in recognizing that images are learned from the media, what images have you picked up from this powerful source?

This chapter has not answered these questions for you. The goal, instead, has been to help you to consider the kinds of influences created and shown by the media—to help you question its intentions so that you may become a better consumer of sexual information.

SELECTED REFERENCES

Brissett, Dennis, and Lewis, Lionel S. "Guidelines for Marital Sex: An Analysis of Fifteen Popular Marriage Manuals." *Family Coordinator* 19 (January 1970): 41–48.

Broderick, Carlfred B. et al. "Do Marriage Manuals Do More Harm Than Good?" *Medical Aspects of Human Sexuality* 4 (October 1970): 50–63.

Gadpaille, W. J. "Male 'Physique' Magazines." *Medical Aspects of Human Sexuality* 5 (April 1971): 45–61.

Geise, L. Ann. "The Female Role in Middle-Class Women's Magazines from 1955 to 1976: A Content Analysis of Nonfiction Selections." *Sex Roles: A Journal of Research* 5 (February 1979): 51–62.

Gordon, Michael. "Sex Manuals: Past and Present." *Medical Aspects of Human Sexuality* 5 (September 1971): 20–37.

Gordon, Michael, and Shankweiler, Penelope J. "Different

Equals Less: Female Sexuality in Recent Marriage Manuals." *Journal of Marriage and the Family* 33 (August 1971): 459–466.

Grotjahn, Martin. "Sex and the Mystery Story." *Medical Aspects of Human Sexuality* 6 (March 1972): 126–140.

Key, William Bryan. *Subliminal Seduction: A Media's Manipulation of a Not so Innocent America.* New York: NAL, 1973.

Lewis, Lionel S., and Brissett, Dennis. "Sex as Work: A Study of Avocational Counseling." *Social Problems* 15 (1967): 8–18.

Lull, James T.; Hanson, Catherine A.; and Marx, Michael J. Recognition of Female Stereotypes in TV Commercials. *Journalism Quarterly* 54 (Spring 1977): 153–157.

Peterson, Gail Beaton, and Peterson, Larry R. "Sexism in the Treatment of Sexual Dysfunction." *Family Coordinator* 22 (October 1973): 397–404.

Pietrofesa, John J., and Pietrofesa, Diane W. "Human Sexuality in the Schools." *Journal of Research and Development in Education* 10 (Fall 1976): 5–12.

Pingree, Suzanne; Hawkins, Robert Parker; Bulter, Matilda; and Paisley, William. "A Scale for Sexism." *Journal of Communication* 26 (Autumn 1976): 193–200.

Rubenstein, Judith S.; Watson, Fletcher G.; and Rubinson, Howard G. "An Analysis of Sex Education for Adolescents by Means of Adolescents' Sexual Interests." *Adolescence* 47 (Fall 1977): 293–311.

Scott, Joseph E., and Franklin, Jack L. "Sex References in the Mass Media." *Journal of Sex Research* 9 (August 1973): 196–205.

Sonenschein, David, and Ross, Mark J. M. "Sex Information in the 'Romance' and 'Confession' Magazines." *Medical Aspects of Human Sexuality* 5 (August 1971): 136-159.

Stauffer, John, and Frost, Richard. "Male and Female Interest in Sexually-Oriented Magazines." *Journal of Communication* 26 (Winter 1976): 25-30.

Venkatesan, M., and Losco, Jean P. "Women in Magazine Ads: 1959-1971." *Journal of Advertising Research* 15 (October 1975): 49-54.

Winick, Charles. "Sex and Advertising." *Sexual Behavior* 1 (April 1971): 36-40, 62-64, 79.

Zube, Margaret. "Changing Concepts of Morality: 1948-1969." *Social Forces* 50 (March 1972): 385-393.

chapter 9
EXPERT
SEXPRESSIONS

Here's a dilemma for you. These five professionals sit at a table: a physician, a minister, a social worker, a psychologist, and a business man. You are given the opportunity to spend thirty minutes with one of these people to ask questions about the facts or fiction of male and female sexuality. Which person do you select? Which person do you feel is best qualified to answer your questions? Which person do you consider the sexual expert? In many cases, none of these people would be more qualified than any other. In fact, it may surprise you to find out later which ones are probably least trained to answer questions about the dynamics of sexuality.

Then how does one become identified as a sex expert? Well, aside from the several jokes running around in your head about practice making perfect, it is a relatively simple matter. Receive a diploma in one of the several fields, hang out a shingle (signifying almost any degree will do), open an office, and, we, the public, are likely to proclaim, "Eureka! A sex expert!" You'll notice that I didn't indicate any training or qualifications. I am merely suggesting that we signify expertise through our expectations.

Who, then, receives our badge of confidence? On whom do we bestow the dubious honor? Physicians, counselors, social workers, and a variety of others, that's who. The question is, why? More times than not, their training in human sexuality is lacking. Yet we mistakenly believe that these professionals are well trained to advise us about our sexual problems. This poorly informed idea often leads to unfortunate consequences—a fool's paradise. And this unwarranted idea may be hazardous to your health, your well-being, and your pride.

How would you feel about asking an intimate question of someone whom you perceive as an expert? For most people, the reality becomes almost too intimidating, too threatening. It takes courage to ask an authority figure a sexual question. That is partly because we haven't learned to describe or discuss our sexual concerns. Besides, we often ask ourselves, "Aren't we supposed to know these answers already?"

You may wonder, "What if they laugh at me?" or say, "They might even think I'm stupid." On the other side, you ask, "What if they can't help after I've taken the big step to get an answer?"

One negative or unhelpful experience with a professional is all it takes for most people simply to give up on the problem entirely. If a professional can't help, we tend to feel that it is our fault—not the professional's fault. There must be something wrong with us; the expert couldn't be at fault. "Well," we conclude, "It really doesn't matter. I was silly to ask such an insignificant thing anyway." Rarely do we think of taking the question or problem to a more qualified person. "So what?" we say.

Consider an experience shared with me by a woman who told of this encounter with a professional. The husband wanted and expected oral sex for himself. Yet returning the same pleasure to his wife seemed to be quite a different thing—somehow not right. Using his tongue on her clitoris or vaginal opening was a turn-off. Earlier conversations about males who did such things impressed upon him that it was a disgusting act. A real man would not do that.

Although the wife felt embarrassed about discussing this openly with her husband, much less with a third person, she decided to seek an expert's insights. After much hesitation, she asked the professional for information and advice. Unfortunately, the husband's ungrounded attitude was supported. Furthermore, inaccurate information presented by the supposedly trained and qualified person upheld the husband's view. The perceived expert explained that the vaginal area was too close to the anus. Therefore, he mistakenly concluded that such an act was indeed unclean. Since the male suffered no such impediment, however, she could continue to provide oral sex for her husband.

What a harmful situation! Inaccurate information continues to reinforce the husband's existing negative image of female sexuality. An opportunity to encourage a more positive and sharing relationship went unnoticed. Instead, negative feelings and interactions between this couple were reinforced.

An isolated incident, you say? Not at all. Professionals carry on the traditions set forth and lived by through providing false information. Why does it happen?

You and I are partly responsible for such professional incompetence. Why? Because of our sins of omission. That seems a fairly harsh indictment, doesn't it? Yet, as a rule, you have identified certain people as sexual experts, even though they may not feel comfortable in that role. They may not want that role. They may not wish to be expected to advise you. But how can they say so without losing your confidence in other areas? Moreover, what skills or qualifications have you demanded?

Sexual knowledge comes from the same sources for both the client or patient and the professional. And it develops for the most part through osmosis—that is, by cultural mingling or absorption. Although many correct facts are learned in the natural process, more complex feelings and behaviors are assimilated through reactions about ourselves and about members of the opposite sex. Monkey see; monkey do. In order to change false impressions, more reliable details are necessary. If there is no change in information, there can be no change in beliefs. Therefore, training is very much needed. Physician (and other professionals), heal thyself—first, please.

Basically, in order to help you, they must be aware of the need for training. They must look into themselves for sexual biases, stereotypes, and possible misrepresentations of facts. This introspection is not easy for any of us, but it is often more difficult for professionals because their self-worth and reputation are based on what they know, not on what they need to know. And because human sexuality is considered so basic, the professional feels indignant about suggestions for additional awareness about what he or she perceives as a fundamental area. Often, professionals don't know that they don't know. Therefore, we must expect and demand that their education include sexual information.

Each of us would like to have sexual questions answered at one time or another. Not everyone, however, can find effective help. Few professionals are properly trained to help. This must change, and it can change. A primary step is adequate training.

TRAINING—WHAT TRAINING?

Ask yourself these questions: Where would you go for an answer to a sexual question or problem? Do you know someone who is qualified? Do you know someone who possesses the trained sensitivity to warrant your confidence? Your answers are probably "no," "no," and "no," unless you are thinking about the very few, such as William Masters and Virginia Johnson. Yet, for even the simplest concern, there may be no one in your own community who qualifies as competent.

Think about the irony for a moment. You live in the day of the expert. If you don't believe me, get out your canceled checks for the past year. There are beauty experts, health experts, tax experts, housing experts, decorating experts, transportation experts, service-repair experts, and reducing experts, to name only a few.

Yet where are the sex experts? Did you know that there is little difference in the amount of training received by current experts and that of nineteenth-century professionals? Surprising, isn't it? While society devotes so much time to sexual curiosity, expression, and experience, the so-called experts remain basically untrained to assist in the resulting anxieties and problems.

You probably haven't given much thought to the sexual training of professionals. That's because we tend to view the people we trust as qualified. Yet giving sexual advice is a serious task. Doing more harm than good is a rather high possibility because of the many myths and fallacies. Doesn't it seem, then, that sexual training should be an important part of the educational process for those who are considered experts? With the accolades go responsibilities and skills.

Of course, sexual experts do exist somewhere, don't they? Think about it for a moment. What professional group would you consider as a reliable source? In order to answer that question, you may want to know that there are basically two kinds of sexual experts available: the indirect sources, such as researchers who provide statistics about sexuality or scientists who investigate questions concerning the reproductive system, and the direct sources, such as psychologists, physicians, and religious leaders who talk with you about sexuality.

In the past, we turned to God and to His direct agents, the religious leaders, to know what we should do about sexual decisions. Now, we often turn to the indirect sources of scientists and educators in order to learn what everyone else is doing so that we know how to behave like peas in a pod—not by commandments but, rather, by statistics. Surveys and studies presented by psychologists, sociologists, and medical personnel provide information for comparing sexual attitudes and behaviors. We can, thereby, follow the mainstream. If we live by science, we want to interact in terms of scientific evaluations of ourselves.

In many ways, we have misused the sexual numbers collected by the data experts. We attempt to apply that information to tell us how we should interact. We use numbers to establish our communications and behaviors. We use numbers to make our sexual decisions. We can learn to paint by numbers, but we can't learn to make love by numbers.

What the data experts do, they tend to do well. Those trained in numbers, however, aren't trained to deal with interactional needs and answers. Those people aren't the experts to help you make decisions, to provide understanding about the facts of life, or to teach you to communicate honestly about your sexual needs. Statistical experts aren't trained as guides or resources for sexual decisions. They would be the first to tell you so.

Again, we look to science for sexual experts because it has given us methods to control procreation that were never dreamed possible. The pill, artificial insemination, test tube babies, and modern abortion procedures can encourage or discourage pregnancy. Take your choice; make your decisions privately: No one need know. Birth control has arrived in this mechanized, scientific age. It solves one problem for only one aspect of your sexuality. But what do those experts offer you before and after your birth control decisions are made? As you know, many sexual anxieties are unrelated to this issue. Yet birth control isn't the beginning and the end to your sexual needs. It's an answer, but it's not the only answer.

Indirect sexual expert sources make strong contributions to your sexual well-being. These are very well trained people in their areas. However, they do not answer the communication aspects. For these concerns, you require a direct sexual expert source. Unfortunately, these people are not equally well trained.

If you want to see direct-source professionals stutter and shuffle, ask what training they've had in personal sexual awareness or sexual counseling. The answer is fairly predictable. Most have not had any training, courses, or workshops. Others have had perhaps one hour, one all-day session or, less likely, one course. Imagine learning everything necessary in one easy hour! Impossible. It may interest you to know that many seminaries offer more information to their ministerial students than is received by students of psychology, sociology, or medicine. Yet we tend to grant the latter rather than the former professionals higher credibility in sexual matters.

For the most part, professionals regret their lack of training, and graduate and professional schools regret not giving their students more training. Nevertheless, the student has so many demands on his or her time that the cry is "Priorities!" As a result, guess what goes first? Human sexuality—a second cousin twice removed.

Currently, the "second cousin" is being invited to more family gatherings. Whereas suggestions for seminars in various professional schools and agencies in the past were met with "Mmm, that is an interesting idea," people are presently giving a second glance toward the need for greater involvement in sexual awareness and training.

But put yourself in the place of the professional who hasn't had training—the professional who has already completed school. Your patients or clients depend on you. They respect you. They believe in your intelligence and your abilities. Feels good, huh? What do you do, then, with the sexual problems of these people who assume that you are an expert in this area? You do what a majority of professionals who are labeled experts do. You put on the mantle of expert. Yet you rely on the same information sources as those who taught your clients and patients—that is, information received from parents, peers, and the media. And, therefore, you are prone to the same myths and fallacies. And on it goes. You don't mean harm. Yet the myths and fallacies become the gospel. They hear the word from the expert—you. Can you see, quite clearly, then, that the expert needs help?

The first step for the professional is awareness. Without an awareness of his or her shortcomings and skills, the professional inadvertently hinders rather than helps. For example, a physician who teaches medical students declared his surprise over lunch one day that I could seriously believe that women possess a similar sexual drive to that of men. Needless to say, I was equally surprised that he believed the opposite. Unknowingly, he described his own sexual attitudes and experiences. This attitude influences his coital relationship with his wife. More importantly, it influences his counseling with patients. Furthermore, these attitudes are passed on to his students. This one individual continues to transmit a spiral of sexual misinformation. Although he would be alarmed to think that he might make a wrong diagnosis, he has no such concerns about sexual advice. A serious offense, no doubt—and one that certainly needs to be changed. How? By awareness. In order to help you, the professional must be aware of his or her own sexual images and attitudes.

Although many professionals recognize that they are ill-prepared to deal with sexual problems, others proceed without caution into the muddled waters. They must become aware of the need for adequate training. We must demand increased skills in this area. Otherwise, they intentionally or unintentionally pass on their biases and problems to you. Ask yourself the question again, "Where could I go for an answer to a sexual question or problem?" Considering the lack of training of many direct sexual expert sources, locating a qualified person seems to be a bit of a task, doesn't it?

PHYSICIANS: THE MOST POPULAR SEX EXPERTS

Picture a kindly, caring family physician listening in rapt attention to the sobbing young bride's sexual problems for thirty minutes. A moving scenario, but it is not likely to happen, is it? First of all, what physician has thirty minutes to sit with one patient? Equally important, how many physicians are prepared or qualified to help effectively?

Interestingly enough, physicians are often the experts with the least training about sexual concerns. Yet they tend to be our first choice for the most qualified professional.

It's a problem of association. They are certainly the experts for medical problems associated with the reproductive system, such as birth control or functional disorders, but what about problems outside the medical realm? That is quite a different story. Physiology is only one possible reason for sexual problems.

It's widely accepted that the majority of sexual problems are psychological rather than physical. Some estimates run as high as ninety-nine percent. The problems tend to be those of communication rather than those related to functional disorders. Therefore, why do so many people confide in physicians about sexual problems? The physician is rarely trained to handle communicative or emotional problems related to sexuality adequately. Yet more and more patients seek the physician's help in these matters: Our belief in their abilities ranges from problems concerning men who have impotence difficulties related to anxieties, to women who don't experience orgasms because they are tense, to parents who want someone to tell little Billy or Susie the facts of life. These and other difficulties are heard every day by the physician, who has neither the time nor the training to help. This must be particularly frustrating for the conscientious physician.

How did physicians inherit the distinction of becoming sexual experts? Why are we so willing to confide in them about sexuality? What is there about these professionals that brings about such trust from us?

Medicine is a highly respected profession—one which stresses the strict confidentiality of the doctor-patient relationship. Sometimes, however, with respect to the patient's sexual anxieties, physicians are known to take such problems less than seriously. This may be due in part to a lack of awareness or training about his or her own sexual biases, stereotypes, and ideas.

I remember a classic example from my earlier days as a surgical nurse. The patient had been put to sleep for a minor vaginal surgical procedure. Scarcely after she was under the anesthetic, the physician repeated a conversation that had occurred the night before between the woman and himself. She explained, rather embarrassed and stammering, that her husband's penis was small. She was wondering, well, hoping, that the operation, in addition to its necessary physical repairs, might also make her vaginal canal smaller. The physician broke up in laughter at that point in the story, and he never told us his reply.

What seemed to him a humorous anecdote was a problem to that couple. Through greater understanding of his own attitudes, and with training in sexual counseling, this physician could have made a positive difference in this couple's relationship. Instead, we can guess that he had few skills to hear what the woman was actually saying. We can also guess that the patient will not seek help from anyone else. Hence, the problem may never be satisfactorily resolved.

The physician probably conveyed the situation as a humorous story because when others laughed he proved that it was, indeed, a frivolous matter rather than a serious problem. It relieved his embarrassment. But had he been taught the necessary communication skills, the event would not have been used to amuse several people.

Physicians are also viewed as sexual experts because they are the professionals in society who are given contact with the most intimate parts of the body. We feel awkward and even threatened exposing our bodies to someone we hardly know. Some patients literally try to hide from the emotional discomfort. One female patient wears sunglasses the day of her pelvic examination—before, during, and after. All day she hides behind the dark glasses because the procedure is emotionally upsetting. This kind of vulnerability necessitates full confidence in the physician.

We also know that modesty is a bit difficult to attain with the physician—yet we keep trying. One physician, while trying to relax a patient during the pelvic exam, asked about her mother, who was also his patient. "How can you even talk about my mother at a time like this?" she demanded sharply. Her feelings of the indecency went further than the simple physical discomfort; she was seeking emotional modesty and comfort as well.

To place ourselves in a situation that is, at the least, a mild inconvenience requires that we view that person as fully knowledgeable about our bodies. We translate this knowledge to a competence in all areas of sexuality. Permitting a physician the inspection and care of the body may not justify confiding the most intimate details of your sexual experiences. The physical and emotional problems about our bodies are often quite different to handle and to give advice about. Nevertheless, we want physicians to convey complete authority about the care of our bodies. It is important to us to perceive them as all-knowing. Our expectations rise far above anything humanly possible. This god-like image is also taken on by them in order to help them to make life and death decisions. Confidence is essential—yet it can be costly, too.

They must see themselves as the best of the best—a belief that is instilled in the student throughout medical school. This is somewhat in contrast to a previous image presented to medical students. Some years ago, the general medical school philosophy taught that students were nothing until the hallowed professors molded and, it was hoped, made them fit to be included among the ranks. Now, they are more frequently considered, from the onset, as members of the elite.

Two years ago, I heard a medical school dean give his welcoming address to the freshman students. On this first day they were told that the hardest part, getting into medical school, was over. They were, now and forever more, the crème de la crème. The medical school personnel, he promised, would do everything possible to help keep them in school.

Once that kind of professional mantle is securely in place, it becomes more difficult to say, "I don't know." We, their patients and clients, expect them always to know—always to have an answer for every problem. They become, in our eyes, far wiser than the overseeing parent. We expect from them the omniscience of God. The final tragedy is that because we expect it and because they are taught it, they come to believe that it "should" be true. It becomes impossible to admit anything less to colleagues, intimates, or patients. Boxed in in this manner, what is the untrained physician to do when patients ask sexual questions outside his or her medical competence? Think about it for a moment. If it was difficult for you to admit a lack of sexual knowledge while growing up, then realize how much more difficult this admission will be for the physician, who is supposed to maintain a pedestal position. They must stand head and shoulders above others even though, in reality, they are prone to the same anxieties, myths, and sexual problems as everyone else. Taking on the garb of the one who must maintain the ever-present image of complete confidence denies them, however, the same ability to seek the necessary information in order to clear away sexual myths or concerns. Can you begin to see, then, why medical students are often reported to be more conservative about sexual attitudes and behaviors than others of their same age?

It is difficult for them to open up to discuss sexual ideas because their world with colleagues and society in general demands that they maintain a certain image. This attitude was brought home recently in one particular medical school where I presented a workshop on sexual communication. During the ten-minute breaks, a most fascinating ritual took place among all but one of the male medical students. They would dash out the door and stand in small circles, participating in groups that can only be compared to the bravado sexual discussions of young adolescent boys: rowdy, boisterous, and heavily laden with off-color words. It seemed necessary to reaffirm who they were by a ritual that was part of their earlier communicative experience—a comfortable experience that allowed for a certain sexual identification with other males. The male who did not join in the short sessions, by the way, had been trained in human sexuality and had worked in a self-help center for women. The center provided various medical information, counseling, and support systems through classes, workshops, and other programs about female sexuality. Awareness and training make the necessary difference. Which physician would you want to talk to? The trained young doctor-to-be? Or, the untrained and uncomfortable young doctors-to-be? If you picked the former, your odds are about twenty-five to one that you won't be that fortunate.

These very relied-upon individuals must receive training in order to help them overcome their feelings of awkwardness. Sadly, that one workshop was the total sexual training those particular students received during their entire years in medical school. Yes, they will study the reproductive system and the functions of the physical body. Beyond that one day, however, any sexual misconceptions, inaccuracies, and biases that remain will be passed on to their patients—passed on to you.

Human sexuality is too important for the most popular sexual expert to be confined to adolescent myths and stereotypes as the basis of his knowledge. Sufficient personal awareness and training must be given or the mantle of expert must be turned to someone else.

DISPENSING WITH STEREOTYPES

I talk to you through who I am. So does the expert. Ribbons, bows, and dolls for her; jack knives, play guns, and marbles for him. This is the way we distinguish real boys from real girls as they grow up. Unfortunately, we don't permit much change even after we're adults. Girls (or women, as many prefer to be called—for good reasons) and men are still expected to conform to the images of the female as passive and the male as aggressive. And because these ideas are firmly held as appropriate for happiness, people who vary from these accepted ideas often find themselves encountering problems. Those problems are sometimes increased by the experts who made strong efforts to help by teaching the person to conform to stereotypic images. Consider the struggle of Judy and Steve. He was a quiet and somewhat nonassertive person, whereas Judy was the exact opposite. Initially, Steve found her achievements and sense of competition stimulating. He was proud. But as their marriage progressed, she became more and more successful in work, whereas Steve's career changed very little. Judy's many accomplishments seemed more and more unsettling and personally threatening to him. As he began to draw into himself, Judy became more aggressive and tried to draw him out to work on the increasing marriage problems. In their fifteenth year of marriage, they finally agreed to see a marriage counselor. The counselor instructed her to give less time to the career and more time to the marriage. He advised that she was a rather formidable woman and should tone down her assertiveness and ambitions that made Steve's own achievements pale in comparison.

For a while, she tried to apply the counselor's advice. She turned down work loads or projects that required extra efforts or time. As a result, her career sacrifices created feelings of resentment. After six months of counseling, she refused to go any more. It was five years later, and only out of the most desperate sense of need, that Judy and Steve sought the help of another counselor. Fortunately, the new counselor recognized their struggle with stereotypic masculine and feminine roles. Instead of trying to move them toward more acceptable images, he taught them to accept who they were and their own comfortable ways of addressing the world. In many ways, their personalities were the exact opposites of traditional masculinity and femininity. However, once they began to see their difference as okay, the tensions and demands decreased.

Accepting these stereotypes shouldn't be demanded any more; neither should they be used to cure. For the most part, they are simply harmful. Professionals who provide advice through stereotypes are being unfair to their clients or patients. They demand that those seeking advice adhere to images that may make the professional comfortable but that may not be beneficial to the person who requests assistance. Nevertheless, authorities continue to push and cram people into these accepted images. They seem to be saying to the individual, "Just keep trying. You'll be happy once your behavior fits the appropriate mold. Wait and see."

The desire to counsel through stereotypic advice is vividly demonstrated through the studies of Inge Broverman and her co-workers. They have researched the attitudes of many kinds of professionals as well as those of the population in general. Read carefully: Their finding powerfully indicates that the Ph.D. and M.D. mental health clinicians, in their research, view stereotypes as both appropriate and healthy. I believe that you will be a bit surprised about the professional judgments of the healthy male and female characteristics:

> . . . In effect, clinicians are suggesting that healthy women differ from healthy men by being more submissive, less independent, less adventurous, less objective, more easily influenced, less aggressive, less competitive, more excitable in minor crises, more emotional, more conceited about their appearance, and having their feelings more easily hurt.[1]

Consider paying someone to instill this imagery further in your own head. Imagine building a troubled relationship on the basis of this perspective. Imagine talking to a professional

---

[1] Inge Broverman et al., "Sex Role Stereotypes: A Current Appraisal," *Journal of Social Issues* 28 (1972): 70.

who perceives the female as having less objectivity about problems and who believes that she gets her feelings more easily hurt in that relationship. How seriously would you, as a professional, listen to her concerns? Her complaints? Also, think about your reactions as a professional to the male who readily lets it be known that he is rather submissive in nature or that he, indeed, does get his feelings easily hurt (most people do feel hurt in one situation or another). And it seems likely, if a professional advises you along these stereotypic lines, that his or her ideas about sexual needs, drives, and equality will be similarly inclined.

The personality of each of us is different. I may be comfortable with certain traditional stereotypes. Yet trying to mold my behaviors to those of others would be extremely poisoning. The same is true for you. You fit no mold: You are you. To seek advice from someone who has everything tied up in a neat pink or blue bow is ridiculous. It won't work. You are, then, paying for that person to potentially harm you rather than help you.

HOW TO FIND COMPETENT ASSISTANCE

It is time that you stopped giving all of yourself to experts without question. It isn't necessary for you to obey blindly as though there were no alternative. That gives the uncomfortable feeling of being in a bind. Recognize, when consulting a professional about matters of sexual advice, that you pay for those services. That person is employed by you. Because of this, you have the right to be assured that those services are competent.

Don't be afraid to ask questions in order to determine the perspectives or training of the individual. By the simple phrasing of four or five questions, you can generally find out the necessary information. Have confidence. For instance, you might begin with a statement similar to this: "My problem (or question) concerns sexuality. As a point of information, naturally I'm interested in the kind of training you've had in this area." If he or she becomes irritated by your statement, that individual probably wouldn't be sensitive to your needs anyway.

Don't allow yourself to feel helpless in finding qualified assistance. You have both the right and the ability to get effective advice. Don't become intimidated by the diplomas on the wall or by the title, "Doctor." Have confidence that you can interview this person briefly in order to ascertain rather quickly whether you wish to continue or not.

Another way to learn more about your sexuality is to enroll in one of the many human sexuality courses being offered by colleges and universities across the country. Read the brief course description, meet the instructor, and attend a session or two. Many of these courses combine biological and relational information. Obviously, you want a discussion course rather than a lecture course.

Many consciousness groups for men and women are also available. Sexual issues are often discussed as some part of the meetings. Examine their purposes and goals as well as their structures and sponsors. A word of caution: Often times these turn out to be gripe sessions about the opposite sex. Such groups can do more harm than good. Again, you may have to investigate several groups in order to find one that seems to fit your particular needs and criteria. These groups are often without cost, and they may be either ongoing or short term. A very good possibility (although difficult to locate) is a group that includes both males and females. We really need to start talking to each other, don't you agree?

Enable yourself to seek assistance, personal growth, or problem solving if you would like to. Don't tell yourself that a sexual problem isn't important enough to merit seeking help. Don't believe that it will always work itself out: Maybe it will, maybe not. If it is a concern that keeps recurring, why not talk to someone?

And don't put a guilt trip on yourself by believing that

a request for sexual advice says that you aren't the man or woman you ought to be. Each of those ideas may poison your sexual pleasure. If there is a possibility that talking to someone makes you feel better, then why not do it? As for feeling that you are less a man or woman for needing help, we all live in a sharing world. Sometimes we give assistance to others, and sometimes we need to reach out and have someone help us.

Decide to be honest with yourself and to admit that sexuality is important to you. You want it to be the best emotional and physical experience possible. You deserve it. Having a question or problem answered can make a difference to you. There are competent people out there to help provide those answers. Should the occasion arise, find that qualified professional to help.

SELECTED REFERENCES

Ahrons, Constance R. "Counselors' Perceptions of Career Images of Women." *Journal of Vocational Behavior* 8 (April 1976): 197–207.

Bear, Sheryl; Berger, Michael; and Wright, Larry. "Even Cowboys Sing the Blues: Difficulties Experienced by Men Trying to Adopt Nontraditional Sex Roles and How Clinicians Can Be Helpful to Them." *Sex Roles: A Journal of Research* 5 (April 1979): 191–198.

Brecher, Edward M. "Krafft-Ebing vs. Havelock Ellis: Contrasting Attitudes in Two Pioneering Students of Sexual Behavior. *Medical Aspects of Human Sexuality* 7 (July 1973): 146–154.

———. *The Sex Researchers.* Boston: Little, Brown, 1969.

Broverman, Inge K. et al. "Sex-Role Stereotypes: A Current Appraisal." *Journal of Social Issues* 28 (1972): 59–78.

———. "Sex Role Stereotypes and Clinical Judgments of Mental Health." *Journal of Counseling and Clinical Psychology* 34 (February 1970): 1–7.

Chesler, Phyllis. "Women and Psychiatrics and Psychotherapeutic Patients." *The Journal of Marriage and the Family* 33 (November 1971): 746–759.

Christensen, Harold T., ed. *Handbook of Marriage and the Family.* Chicago: Rand McNally, 1964.

Coombs, Robert H. "Inhibition in Verbal Sexual Communication." *Medical Aspects of Human Sexuality* 5 (April 1971): 152–163.

———. "Sex Attitudes of Physicians and Marriage Counselors." *Family Coordinator* 20 (July 1971): 269–277.

Ditzion, Sidney. *Marriage, Morals, and Sex in America: A History of Ideas.* New York: Octagon Books, 1969.

Fabian, Judith. "The Role of the Therapist in the Process of Sexual Emancipation." *Psychiatric Opinion* 10 (August 1973): 31–33.

Frank, Irving, and Frank, Rosanne K. "Problems of Sexuality as Encountered in a General Family Practice." *Psychosomatics* 14 (July 1973): 230–232.

Gochros, Harvey L. "Sexual Problems in Social Work Practice." *Social Work* 16 (January 1971): 3–5.

Gottheil, Edward, and Freedman, Abraham. "Sexual Beliefs and Behaviors of Single, Male Medical Students." *Journal of the American Medical Association* 212 (May 1970): 1327–1332.

Klein, Viola. *The Feminine Character: History of an Ideology.* 2d ed. Urbana: University of Illinois Press, 1972.

McCary, James L. "Human Sexuality: Past, Present, and Future." *Journal of Marriage and Family Counseling* 4 (April 1978): 3–12.

Money, John. "The Development of Sexology as a Discipline." *Journal of Sex Research* 12 (May 1976): 83–87.

Pauly, Ira B. "Influence of Training and Attitudes on Sexual Counseling in Medical Practice." *Medical Aspects of Human Sexuality* 6 (March 1972): 84–92.

Pauly, Ira B., and Goldstein, Steven G. "Physicians' Ability to Treat Sexual Problems." *Medical Aspects of Human Sexuality* 4 (October 1970): 24–49.

——. "Physicians' Attitudes Toward Premarital and Extramarital Intercourse." *Medical Aspects of Human Sexuality* 5 (January 1971): 32–45.

Peplau, Letitia Anne, and Hammen, Constance L. "Social Psychological Issues in Sexual Behavior: An Overview." *Journal of Social Issues* 33 (1977): 1–6.

Petras, John W. *Sexuality in Society.* Boston: Allyn & Bacon, 1973.

Riegel, Robert E. *American Women: A Story of Social Change.* Cranbury, N.J.: Associated University Presses, 1970.

Sayad, Robert M. "A Perspective of Sexual Therapy." *Family Life* 38 (November–December 1978): 2–12.

Sheppe, William M. "The Family Physician and Human Sexuality." *Medical Aspects of Human Sexuality* 6 (July 1972): 11–29.

Woods, Sherwyn M. "Sexual Problems of Medical Students." *Medical Aspects of Human Sexuality* 6 (February 1972): 66–85.

part three

Sexpressions:

COMMUNICATION AND SEXUAL DISCOVERY

chapter 10
THE LANGUAGE OF COITUS

Your language shapes your sexuality. An interesting thought. But let me give you an example of what I mean. Have you wondered why the percentage of female orgasms has steadily increased since the early part of this century? A change in biology? No. A change in language.

Your language forms and reveals sexuality. The who, what, when, where, and how of sexuality are each shaped by language. Yet do you realize what language says? Are you aware of its effects on you? Do you know its importance to your sexual well-being? Although you may take language for granted, most of your sexual behavior is determined by language.

If you believe that sexuality is based primarily upon physical responses, look again. Language influences sexuality through the acceptance and use of words, gestures, symbols, and signals. Language is you. Thoughts, actions, and responses conform to your relationship with language. And your language can be a sexual handicap.

Language shapes sexuality and sexuality shapes language. Normal body processes, such as male and female orgasms, are affected by attitudes expressed through language. Nineteenth-century women, for example, learned that the good woman is a sexless woman. The powerful consequence of that message becomes devastatingly clear. Negative messages, negative responses.

Again, consider the differences in perceived successes or failures of the nineteenth- and the twentieth-century male. Today's male is looked upon as a failure when premature ejaculation occurs. In the past century, however, "faster than a speeding bullet" seemed ideal. A decent woman was supposed to be grateful for such a male. What, then, brought about the turn around in these male and female responses?

One difference is language. The language of coitus is changing, and these changes influence sexuality. What is or isn't considered acceptable or appropriate becomes an active part of your sexual language. The following examples of Cindy and Beverly will help to give fuller understanding to the importance of language. You will identify, in some degree, with the communication problems of one or both people. Certain situations or events bring out coital bravado or inhibitions in each of us.

Cindy's coital language is fashioned for show: The verbal and nonverbal language hides certain insecurities. Her coital manners are swinging and free but lack intimacy. Intimacy is scary, so language discourages closeness. Salty street language combined with a masked nonchalance create the message, "Don't get close."

As one relationship after another fails to produce a sharing experience, she defensively develops the following attitude: "Men are uncaring, unemotional, manipulative bastards." She doesn't see that her language denies others the chance to get close.

For Cindy, eliminating the bravado language would strip her down to a scared, hurt little girl. Honest language would create honest relationships, but she is afraid to reveal who she is. Many of us share this concern with Cindy. It is frightening to reveal the real you. As one writer explains, we are afraid to tell others who we are because if that is not accepted, then we have nothing left.

Yet sometimes our fears are so close that we cannot hide them. Beverly is such a person. She tried to hide embarrassments about sexual conversations and situations. The discomfort and awkward feelings nevertheless show in her walk, in her talk, in her lovemaking. She very much wants to feel spontaneous and secure and react with less anxiety. She tried. She tells herself, "I will act differently," but she remains unsuccessful in making changes. Recently, however, she has initiated sessions with a counselor who understands the importance of language. They discuss her images and relationships about sexual concepts and roles. As a result, these awarenesses allow her to become less inhibited and more at ease. Changing her relationship with language is making a difference.

There are parts of Cindy and Beverly in you—both the bravado and the inhibitions. The bravado causes abruptness or brashness when you want and desire intimacy. Or, through those inhibitions, you react with reserve when you want to feel unrestricted and expressive.

Think about your own language. Begin to notice how words and concepts convey or construct coital attitudes and behaviors. How do your experiences with language define your sexuality? Consider your attitudes toward the following:

1. Words, phrases, and attitudes about males and females who do or don't participate in the act of coitus. Include attitudes that relate to the double standard, the good-bad woman image, masculinity-femininity, and so on.
2. Words used to describe sexual body processes: hard-on, erection, orgasm, coming, menstruation, being on the rag, and so on.

3. Attitudes about the who, what, when, where, how, and why of coitus.
4. Words used to describe the act of coitus: making love, screwing, balling, scoring, and the like.
5. Words used to describe males and females: gals, guys, chicks, dudes, cunts, studs, women, men, and so on.
6. Words that describe images of males and females who participate in coitus: stud, whore, nymphomaniac, frigid bitch, tease, and so on.
7. Words used for body parts: cunt, prick, penis, family jewels, tits, breasts, ass, and so on.
8. Words used for coital activity or positions: dog fashion, 69, missionary fashion, oral sex, giving head, cunnilingus, fellatio, and so on.
9. Expressions during the act of coitus: sighs, moans, requests, and so on.
10. Nonverbal communications during coitus through movement, touch, and facial and body expressions.

Your language reflects childlike joy and mischievous affection or distrust, anxiety, and hostility. Language also expresses a need to protect, defend, insult, hurt, enjoy, manipulate, fear, respect, pleasure, perform, fantasize, and joke. You create and live a language of coitus. The manner in which language is used and experienced affects your sexuality. Language reveals who you are and how you want to be seen.

What you say and how you say it can determine your coital responses and pleasures. You have designed a language of coitus that has become the means of transmitting and announcing your sexuality. You define yourself and your relationships with others by using that language. Your communicative effectiveness often determines the degree of your sexual happiness.

Because this society doesn't encourage direct and honest

language, the potential for miscommunication or problem communication is considerable. Honest, open communication is looked upon as risky, even with those we most trust. Flirting, innuendoes, and guessing games are more often preferred because the risk of rejection or hurt seems less likely. We believe that the less we reveal, the less we will be hurt. What actually tends to result is that we form protective language habits that isolate us from our feelings. Because of these habits, we lose the ability to express our real needs. A partner, then, must guess our needs or feelings. He or she has to interpret cues of anger or frustration by hunch or guess. Most people, by guessing, will miss as many cues as they catch. Why is it necessary for intimates to guess?

Even the simple desire to have coitus is often restricted to hints and ploys rather than being communicated openly. Imagine, then, the difficulties encountered with more subtle concerns. How do you convey the need to be held close or cuddled? How do you express the desire to do something you learned was vulgar or something that provoked ribald jokes? When you feel something is lacking within the coital relationship, how is that communicated? How do you handle irritation or disappointment when your partner will or won't say or do something for you?

Most of us say very little to our coital partners about what goes on in bed. You hope that problems or frustrations will work themselves out. You tell yourself that talking about such things only makes matters worse. Remember, however, that often little coital annoyances or needs left untended have a way of interfering with or disrupting that relationship. Those annoyances may be reflected in gradual boredom, lack of interest, problems in getting or staying excited, and so on.

Don't leave something as important as coital communication to chance. Learn to promote better relationships and self-images by effective communication. By reading about problems in the language of coitus, you can gain insight and confidence that may contribute to greater sexual pleasures.

THE COITAL LANGUAGE OF SHOULDS

One word, "should," predicts failure as you seek sexual happiness. This word and its compatriot friends, "must" and "ought," guarantee the failure of even the most positive intentions. Part of the reason that you are bound to lose is the hidden clause linked with "should." Your mind recognizes and accepts the spoken or unspoken phrase. It is the hidden clause rather than the "should" to which you respond. Unaware of this, you try and try to work through the "should." More often than not, you fail. Consider this example: "I should lose weight in order to be more attractive, but . . ."

What you say after the but is the hidden clause that shows your real attitude or behavior. Look at a different statement for additional clarity: "She is a nice person, but she gets on my nerves."

The real message is found in the "but" clause. Disregard anything before "but." Actually, the first clause merely sets up a reference for the point of concern.

Another hidden clause attached to should is "because." "I should feel, or act, or become, because . . ." The because tells you, ". . . because people will not like me if I do" or ". . . because people will not like me if I don't." Or it says, ". . . because other people do" or ". . . because other people don't."

Both of these hidden clauses—"but" and "because"—are detrimental. They short-circuit what you are. Instead of reinforcing what may be good for you, they demand that the standards of others take priority.

You are you. Decide for yourself. Be responsible for

your behavior, not for that of others. Focus on the experiences that are good for you. How can you know? How can you decide? Simply identify the "but" or "because" clause connected to the "should" statement. Look at some of the more common statements that we feed ourselves about sexuality: Stop after each statement and say to yourself, not "but" or "because"—*why*.

1. I should lose weight.
2. I should have an orgasm.
3. I should last longer during the sex act.
4. I should become more sexually excited or excitable.
5. I should be certain my partner has an orgasm.
6. We should make love in the dark.
7. We should make love more often.

Now examine the "should nots":

1. I should not lose an erection so easily.
2. I should not fantasize about such things as . . .
3. I should not concentrate so much on having an orgasm.
4. I should not get turned-off so easily.

Where are these and other statements embossed in gold or written in the sky; are they mottoes of universal truth? Where is it written on a sacred tablet of truth that you must abide by these statements? You may say that it is to your pleasure and advantage to become or to experience certain "shoulds" or "should nots." Possibly. You may choose to make those decisions. Furthermore, you may feel that accomplishing the "should" represents substantial gains for you. That is all well and good if it helps you to feel good and comfortable. The indispensable consideration is that you like yourself, regardless of the choice.

Look what happens with "should." "I should lose weight."

The corollary is "I will not like myself until, or unless, I lose weight." Or, "I should have an orgasm" becomes "I am not a complete person unless I have an orgasm." Couples often see themselves failing as a result of oppressive "shoulds." "We should make love more often" becomes "Because we don't make love more often, there is something wrong with the relationship."

Accepting a sexual "should" grants you the power to whittle down self-acceptance and self-confidence. A "should" draws on past experiences or problems. It restricts your ability to deal with the present and the future. The following problems are identified with the "should":

1. It puts into your mind all the people who told you that the "should" was true, those who reinforced the "should."
2. It programs you to behave according to the precepts of the "should."
3. It forces you to act out of habit and not desire.
4. It has the potential of making you feel that you are a failure.
5. It sets up a standard imposed by the standards of others.
6. It kills the sense of individuality by destroying the joy you may take in yourself.
7. It prevents you from concentrating on the act itself—on pleasure. Instead, you concentrate on the standard. Remember, it isn't the standard that will reward you.
8. It makes you resent the people who set the "shoulds" up. Instead of loving the standard, the bearers of "should" become the censors or judges of whether you meet the "shoulds." It creates interference.
9. It blinds you to optional ways of behaving. That's why "shoulds" are so easy to fall into. You cannot see other options.

Why say you should or shouldn't? Who says you shouldn't

enjoy certain aspects of coitus? Who says it's dirty? Not nice? Who says your body isn't terrific because it weighs 100 pounds or 250 pounds? Who says people lose interest in sex after sixty? Who says masturbation is self-abuse? Who says that you should have an erection in thirty seconds? Who says that you don't have enough sex drive?

Decide for yourself. Identify "who says." Make your own decision. Then, invert the "should" clause with the "but" or "because" clause. For example:

> "I should get an erection in thirty seconds because other people do (maybe they do—maybe they don't)."
>
> CHANGE TO
>
> "Other people get an erection in thirty seconds, but I take longer (or I like to take longer)."

Let's look at one more example:

> "I should have an orgasm every time because a real man or woman does."
>
> CHANGE TO
>
> "Other people believe they have failed without orgasm, but I enjoy the pleasure of the excitement."

When the "should" is removed, the statements reflect your own feelings or desires rather than those of others. Removing the "should" lets the experience become the pleasure. Change the language, and you change the experience. The next time you think or say "I should, . . ." ask yourself "Who says I should?" Ask yourself "Why?"

You can learn from the similarities between mental and physical tensions. The next time a "should" occurs, try doing this. Constrict your stomach muscles. Then ask yourself "Am I constricting my abilities to choose in a similar fashion?" Physical and mental constrictions create tension, which reduces your abilities to move with grace, comfort, or pleasure. The coital language of "should" produces a double bind, for it has a way of denying you the ability to do the very thing you would like to do. It restricts. I should, but I can't. The fact is that *you can.*

THE LANGUAGE OF COITAL DUTY

Society creates a language of coital duty. Through this language, you are told what is expected and how to behave. You may turn these expectations into demands. And, remember, an ultimatum rarely leads to a desirable response. More often, it causes problems.

The language of coital duty states "You owe me" or "You owe the relationship." It says, in so many words, "I'm not happy because you aren't doing your sexual duty." (Although you may not use the actual word, your expectations imply obligations.) Is this statement of duty your spoken or unspoken dialogue to a lover? If it is, it doesn't create thoughts of passion. Passion, no; passiveness, yes. Which response do you want from your lover? Replacing the language of coital duty with a language of coital desire changes passiveness into passion.

Nineteenth-century language told the female that it was her duty to endure the sexual act. That repressive language of coital duty is passé. Gone for the most part, but not forgotten by some couples. I remember talking to one particularly distressed young woman whose husband became angry when she showed the slightest stirrings of sexual interest. His attitudes reflected past traditions more than present language styles.

Currently, the language of coital duty directs itself to a language of techniques and expertise. This establishes the male's responsibility to stage a four-star performance. Act one, the warm-up; Act two, the main event; Act three, the climax; and Act four, the postcoital intimacies. No more quickies. He must, instead, develop all the intricacies. He must be an acrobat with a variety of coital positions. His timing and coordination must be synchronized so that his penis, hands, feet, and anything else that moves are applied to heighten pleasure by clever and novel exhibitions. He must be imaginative and skillful, and he must put on a winning performance each time because she may be rating him. Who says so? All too many books, magazines, movies, and conversations tell him so.

Paradoxically, the male's duty to be such a sterling performer is matched only by the female's duty to have an orgasm or orgasms. Although it has little effect on the woman whose coital experiences aren't problematic, it sets up a strong potential for failure among women who rarely reach orgasms. The harder she tries to achieve the necessary orgasm, the more elusive it becomes. Yet the elusive orgasm is not really so elusive after all. Women who never experience climax during coitus do have orgasms with a vibrator or by other manual means. Doesn't this tell you that the physiological capacity for orgasm is often not the primary factor? Males and females alike must begin to combat the language of duty so that feelings, responses, and pleasures may be enjoyed to the fullest potential.

When you participate in coitus through duty, you perform an act of obligation. Obligation doesn't make for cuddly sex. The act becomes more a turn-off than a turn-on.

You may be thinking "But I have certain sexual rights, don't I?" Yes, of course you do. However, demanding your sexual rights or demanding sexual change in yourself or in your partner isn't likely to win a blue ribbon of success for either of you. Instead, change your language of coital duty to a softer, more mutual language of desire. You may find a renewal of your lover's participation with you. Notice the difference between the coital language of duty and the coital language of desire. *Duty says,* "It is your duty," which implies, "Either you do this or I'll be angry or sullen; I will cry, go out with other men or women, and so on." Either way, the pressure is on. *Desire says,* "I really feel excited, aroused, pleasured when you. . . ." "That really makes me feel good."

The language of desire gives a compliment and expresses needs and feelings in a positive fashion. Think about it. You prefer to be talked to in which language: duty or desire?

Also, notice that the emphasis is changed from the "You must" to "I feel." Your lover no longer has to experience the burden of guilt or failure. If a particular response or interaction doesn't occur, blame is not given. A couple who wants to enjoy the coital relationship will discard the language of duty—and enjoy the language of desire.

THE COITAL LANGUAGE OF POLARITIES

Males and females are often viewed in terms of language opposites: passive or aggressive; dependent or independent; inferior or superior; weak or strong. When your language accents these and other polarities, your relationship reflects the consequences of polarities. You will think, talk, and react in terms of opposites and differences. Male and female needs and emotions are not different. Society, however, teaches that we must interact as though they are.

Our language creates and reinforces polarities in the sexual dimensions of our relationships. Your acceptance of language polarities requires that the male be the initiator, the more active partner, and that he be characterized by fewer emotional needs. The female, on the other hand, is the respondent, is passive, and has great emotional needs.

Under these circumstances, sharing or mutual decisions about the coital act become difficult. Relating through this language tends to isolate males and females. Furthermore, these interactions do not promote mutual responsibility for pleasurable coitus. To experience the act of coitus believing that each of you acts and reacts differently limits your ability to understand your partner.

It is difficult to be close to someone with whom you feel "less than" or "better than." These interactions demand that you act out those polarities: weak, passive, and dependent or strong, aggressive, and independent. The polarized sexual language inhibits the ability to share your intimate self. It does not allow you to be you.

When you feel distant, isolated, or unable to communicate with your lover, it may be because polarities have led to misunderstandings that, in turn, have built walls between you and your partner. Sit down now and think to yourself, "Do I wait for the other person to initiate the coital act?" "Do I passively accept the coital choices of my lover?" "Do I willingly indicate my preferences?" Or from the other perspective, "Do I feel threatened by the sexual initiative of my partner?" "Do I sometimes ask myself, 'I wonder if she really enjoys what I'm doing—I wish she would let me know!'"

Having a different coital language for males and females hinders honest and effective communication. Developing a language of equality promotes healthy, nourishing self-concepts and relationships. As you make the effort to see yourself and others through a language of equality, you are more free to accept and express yourself. Equality in language fosters respect and trust. It tears down those sexual barriers that the language of polarities helps to build.

THE COITAL LANGUAGE OF SILENCE

Silence can convey the highest expressions of coital enjoyment, or it can be used as a weapon more devastating than any words. Messages, both spoken and silent, are constantly exchanged between you and your partner. For those most eloquent and intimate moments, enjoy and savor each other in silence. But also look to see if you manipulate through silence.

Think of those special, magical times when silent images magnify the beauty and splendor of the moment. Words would only present feeble attempts to describe the feelings. You both understand. The silence and quiet of the moment says it all.

But, at other times, silent images are unclear. And the sensations make you anxious and uneasy. Those unpleasant emotions are further supported by a look, a moving away, a gesture that creates a chilling, invisible wall between you. Perhaps you are the one who is hurt, disappointed, or angry about something that did or did not occur in the coital relationship. You don't want to talk about it. But you do want to communicate your displeasure. You know that silence conveys many of the same emotions said with words. For example, consider the following:

1. I'm hurt.
2. You failed.
3. You're not a good lover.
4. I'm angry.
5. I don't want to (shown by a lack of involvement or interest during coitus).
6. You're an S.O.B.
7. You don't excite me anymore (so I won't be romantic, considerate, etc.).
8. Beg me.
9. It's a physical need—I don't love you.
10. Maybe I'm seeing someone else.

Within the silent language, you mentally move away from the relationship. Although the reason for the displeasure is logical and clear to you, it isn't always evident to your partner. The choice to retreat into a silent language may create a chain reaction where both of you feel more injured. Your partner sees only a negative reaction directed against himself or herself. As you try to communicate through silent behavior, your partner may feel no options except to protect his or her own sense of vulnerability. With little opportunity to resolve conflicts, the situation may continue to affect the coital relationship negatively.

Remember that you can't guess what your partner is thinking. Then, why should he or she know what you are thinking? Your lover can't guess your thoughts.

Why do you expect others to guess? You must verbalize what your thoughts, needs, and frustrations actually are. The silly game of "You know why I'm silent" asks for parlor tricks that few of us can possibly pull off successfully.

Silent images are open to many interpretations. Why play games? Clearly say what your feelings are. Be honest and fair in your expressions. Don't badger or belittle and then expect encouragement and support or understanding to develop. Learn to state your feelings. Not in such a way as to destroy, injure, or retaliate but rather to bring closeness into your relationship. Ask yourself these important questions: "Is my silence for shared moments of intimacy?" and "Am I using silence in a harmful way?"

One word of caution. There may be times when you or your partner are hurt, angry, or resentful and when talking about it immediately would create greater problems. In that case, tell your partner that you feel that time is needed to sort things out. But promise to use that time to think about the situation. Go into another room, take a shower, or go for a walk. Use whatever space and time are necessary to help you to see the situation more clearly. Try to put yourself in your partner's place. Try to see both sides. But then go back and discuss your feelings—not by saying, "You do such and such" but by saying, "My feelings are. . . ." The more you discover your own feelings, the more likely you are to talk to your partner without being tuned out.

DEVELOPING LANGUAGE FOR COITAL WELL-BEING

Now that you've thought about your language, does it reflect sexual well-being or sexual problems? Do you protect feelings of vulnerability through bravado or inhibitions? Do you recognize that certain language changes can promote more positive experiences for you? If you see the influence of language on sexuality, you have taken a big step toward developing a language that builds the coital well-being that you desire.

The following questions will further serve as a guide to help personalize the concepts on coital language. Take several minutes to explore and answer the seven items as honestly as possible.

1. Do I often use words, concepts, and images to mask what I really feel?
2. Do I feel embarrassed about my body? If so, remember that self-esteem and self-concepts are developed through language. Changing the way you talk about yourself is a step toward changing the way you think about yourself.
3. Are my communications to the opposite sex often expressed through feelings of inferiority or superiority?
4. Do I believe that there are far more differences than similarities between the sexes? Make a list. If you find a substantial number of differences, you may be perceiving the other sex as a fearful unknown. What we don't understand, we tend to fear. Honesty will be easier and less threatening as you better understand the similarities as well as the differences.
5. Does my sexual language have more negatives than positives?
6. Does my language restrict what I need or want because of the language of "should" or "duty"?
7. Does my language hold one sex (myself or my partner) more responsible for the success or failure of coitus?

You can learn to communicate more effectively. It requires that you make a conscious effort, but you can learn to use language to provide the pleasure and confidence that you desire. Is it worth the effort? Of course it is. So begin now to experience the difference. And vive la difference.

SELECTED REFERENCES

Aaron, Ruth. "Male Contributions to Female Frigidity." *Medical Aspects of Human Sexuality* 5 (May 1971): 42-57.

Averback, Alfred et al. "How Can Sex Be More Pleasurable?" *Medical Aspects of Human Sexuality* 5 (September 1971): 150-170.

Balswick, Jack O., and **Peek, Charles W.** "The Inexpressive Male: A Tragedy of American Society." *Family Coordinator* 20 (October 1971): 363-368.

Bauman, Karl E. "Selected Aspects of the Contraceptive Practices of Unmarried University Students." *Medical Aspects of Human Sexuality* 5 (August 1971): 76-89.

Bell, Robert R. "Female Sexual Satisfaction as Related to Levels of Education." *Sexual Behavior* 1 (November 1971): 9-14.

Carson, Katherine F. et al. "Should a Man Ask His Sex Partner if She Had an Orgasm?" *Medical Aspects of Human Sexuality* 13 (May 1979): 120-129.

Chilman, Catherine S. "Some Psychosocial Aspects of Female Sexuality." *Family Coordinator* 23 (April 1974): 123-131.

Clark, LeMon. "Is There a Difference Between Clitoral and

Vaginal Orgasm?" *Journal of Sex Research* 6 (February 1970): 25-28.

Coombs, Robert H. "Inhibition in Verbal Sexual Communication." *Medical Aspects of Human Sexuality* 5 (April 1971): 152-163.

Fasteau, Marc Feigen. *The Male Machine.* New York: McGraw-Hill, 1974.

Gadpaille, Warren J. et al. "What Do Women Find Most Difficult to Understand About Men's Sexuality?" *Medical Aspects of Human Sexuality* 13 (January 1979): 69-91.

Gordon, Michael. "Sex Manuals: Past and Present." *Medical Aspects of Human Sexuality* 5 (September 1971): 20-37.

Hunt, Morton. *Sexual Behavior in the 1970's.* Chicago: Playboy Press, 1974.

Jourard, Sidney M. *The Transparent Self.* 2nd ed. New York: D. Van Nostrand, 1971.

Kaye, Harvey E. *Male Survival: Masculinity Without Myth.* New York: Grossett & Dunlap, 1974.

Litewka, Jack. "The Socialized Penis." *Liberation* 18 (March-April 1974): 16-25.

Masters, William H., and Johnson, Virginia E. *Human Sexual Inadequacy.* Boston: Little, Brown, 1970.

Peterson, Gail Beaton, and Peterson, Larry R. "Sexism in the Treatment of Sexual Dysfunction." *Family Coordinator* 22 (October 1973): 92-113.

Powell, John. *Why Am I Afraid to Tell You Who I Am?* Chicago: Argus Communication Company, 1969.

Renshaw, Domeena C. "Sexual Boredom." *Medical Aspects of Human Sexuality* 13 (June 1979): 16–25.

Roth, Nathan. "Sexual Revenge." *Medical Aspects of Human Sexuality* 13 (February 1979): 8–21.

Singer, Irving. *The Goals of Human Sexuality.* New York: W. W. Norton & Company, Inc., 1973.

Stanley, Elizabeth et al. "Can Women Enjoy Sex Without Orgasm?" *Medical Aspects of Human Sexuality* 7 (January 1973): 102–114.

chapter 11
CREATING FACILITATIVE SEXPRESSIONS

Your penis or vagina functions according to the messages you provide. This is sometimes to your delight, other times to your regret. It recognizes, before you do, being threatened, hurt, angry, manipulated, frightened, and so on. When these emotions of vulnerability are sensed, it turns off without consulting you. Although you may not immediately identify those feelings, the penis or vagina isn't fooled. But don't fault your sexual equipment for failure—fault communication instead.

In order to maximize sexual pleasure, develop facilitative communication by constructing skills to improve effective sexual interactions. Doing so provides an A+ in rapport. This enables each of you to have a more successful understanding of the other's needs. Facilitation = pleasure. When you can more clearly express sexual emotions, hurt feelings or avoidances occur less often. The lines of communication aren't likely to get jumbled in a maze of verbal contortions designed to hide your feelings.

Learning facilitative communication improves straight messages: those sent and received. It thereby encourages your sexual equipment to stay in the most cooperative working order. Hidden innuendoes, manipulations, and other dishonest strategies go by the wayside when facilitative communication skills increase. This is because a majority of distrusts and fears come from inside ourselves rather than primarily as a reaction to the other. We fear ourselves and for ourselves.

The need to control decreases as the ability to understand increases. You need less control because you feel more in control: You feel less anxiety, and as your ability to say what you want improves, you are less fearful of others. Your relationship takes on new meanings through facilitative sexpressions toward each other.

But you may ask, "What if I learn to be a more facilitative communicator, but my partner doesn't? What good will that do me?" This is often the case. Listen. You cannot determine other people's behavior—much as you would like to at times. Yet, although you can't control other people's actions, you can control your reactions. Although you are not responsible for other people's actions, you are nevertheless responsible for your own reactions. You are responsible for who you are. Nobody else is: You are. Improve communication skills, and you establish a better feeling about who you are—a better, happier you. Now isn't that worth something, regardless of what your partner does? Besides, a change in you often changes that resistant other.

The importance of facilitative communication cannot be overstressed. It begins with a better understanding of those sexpressions presented in your environment. Examine communications with your parents, your peers, and the media as well. Consider the games you play with the opposite sex. Are they healthy or unhealthy games? Ask yourself whether sexual stereotypes about masculinity and femininity get in the way of your happiness. Look closely at your language. You may find that the language reflects attitudes and habits that hinder your sexuality. Awareness is the first step.

The second step is to develop facilitative ways of communicating and to eliminate harmful patterns. You may currently interact through habits that don't bring the best results. We all fall into certain harmful patterns. The problem is that we don't recognize these problems initially, and often when we do see them, we don't know a better approach.

Remember that you didn't learn those old habits overnight and that you probably won't change them in one swift attempt. New ways of relating feel uncomfortable—stiff and awkward. That will pass, however. As you develop skills, you'll feel more in control, more capable. The more you try to have understanding, the more you actually feel in control.

The following ideas will help you to develop more skillful ways to interact. You gain control by increasing understanding. Certain of these guidelines and concepts are re-emphasized, whereas others are newly presented. Each, however, is a positive way to better sexpressions.

COITAL COMMUNICATION ETIQUETTE: TO MAKE OR KEEP SEX GREAT

When the coital relationship is so good that it can't get better—be sure to keep it that way. Or you may want to bring about certain pleasant improvements. Either way, you want to create or establish good rapport. Good rapport may originally result when you look, touch, hear bells, and see fireworks, but to build a deeper quality depends on your relational skills. Here are several guidelines to ensure the continuance of good experiences or to build toward better experiences through facilitative communication.

1. *Don't assume.* You and your partner aren't mirror images. You have different likes and dislikes, different pleasures, and different needs and wants. Don't assume that your feelings are like his or hers. Don't assume that he or she

knows your feelings. Don't assume that you know what the other person wants, likes, and needs. Make an ongoing part of your relationship the strength of knowing rather than relying on "I think" assumptions. Talk to each other. Ask, don't assume. There's a wide world of difference between assumptions and realities. If you don't believe me, recall the times when you've felt "You only *think* that you know what I want or need." He or she doesn't always know—and neither do you. Don't take that chance. When you make a correct assumption—terrific. When you make a wrong assumption—watch out! Also, remember that assumptions about the other person can be the first step in taking each other for granted.

2. *Be honest but sensitive.* Talking about the sexual relationship with your partner provides a mutually satisfying coital relationship for both of you—one of honesty tempered with sensitivity. It's not permission for rudeness. Nor is it a weapon used to get back, as shown in this attack of honesty: "You want to know what I think of your lovemaking? Well, I'll tell you. You don't know anything!" Is this honesty? Hardly! Look closely. The message in this costume of honesty is retaliation. The honesty you seek brings greater closeness, not greater distance. Speak of things that need to be said. Otherwise, walls build between you. The rule is to express your feelings with the same honesty and sensitivity that you want for yourself.

3. *Don't fake.* Any time you or your partner fake coital responses, or reactions, there is a slight feeling of isolation and less mutuality about the experience. You may believe that your partner feels temporarily better as a result. Perhaps. But the overall effect is detrimental—especially to you. It's make-believe. It's one step back from making love *with* each other. Instead, it's making love *to* each other. When you pretend, the playacting denies both partners. It denies the one who fakes a receiving of plea-

sure, and it also denies the other partner the giving of pleasure. The duality of giving and receiving, of pleasing and being pleased, is terminated.

Don't fake. Learn to experience all the different sensations of the moment rather than concentrating on an academy award performance or the arrival of the conclusion. Imagine enjoying a three-act play if your thoughts were solely concerned with the arrival of the grand finale. You'd miss the enjoyment of the entire experience for the anticipated pleasure of the last five minutes. Sounds foolish, huh? Well, it is frequently concentrating on how things "ought to be" or on "how they are going to be" that leads to faking enjoyment. Don't fake or pretend—enjoy.

4. *Share what turns you on.* When something makes you feel especially good, let your partner know. Why the big secret? He or she can't always guess what pleases you, so don't be bashful about letting him or her know. Don't make a guessing game out of lovemaking. How could you possibly expect him or her to know exactly what you want? Your moods vary, don't they? And when your partner asks what you would like, don't say "I don't care." Do yourself a favor. Give up that euphoric fantasy of the workless passion that happens magically every time. Instead, tell your partner what you want, what you like, and what pleases you and makes you feel good. What you say can be as important as what you do—oftentimes more so.

5. *Share fantasies.* Everybody has exciting fantasies. Why not share those fantasies and even let your lover help you play out the sequence? Naturally, use discretion in revealing certain aspects. If the place, situation, position, and circumstances include the attractive male or female down the street, you obviously know which detail to

omit. Nevertheless, talking about or playing out sexual fantasies often adds another erotic dimension to lovemaking. Why not try it?

6. *Tell your lover what he or she does well.* Most of us compliment people on how well they look, on what they wear, or on their career abilities. Why don't we compliment our lovers on the things they do that bring us good feelings? It's one level of pleasure to experience those touches, caresses, and attentions physically. It's also pleasurable to appreciate verbally certain of his or her skills that make you feel super. (If you think that your lover doesn't have any skills, then help him or her develop some.) If you can't brag to that special person about his or her abilities, with whom can you share such intimate delights and pleasures?

7. *Be sincere.* When you compliment, mean what you say. It builds trust in you and in the relationship. Nobody likes a false sense of security for very long.

8. *Respect the other person's right not to be in the mood.* Nobody is always in the mood. Physical or emotional situations occur, and you or your partner simply don't feel like making love. When that happens, either person should say so. Realize, however, that it is one thing to say, "I'm not in the mood," which has a tone of turning down or rejecting the other person. It has quite a different tone when you say, "I'd rather wait until I can give you my full attention."

And, by the way, the matter of your partner's "coital timing needs" is often a mystery to you. There is a tendency to see the other person as being in the mood too often or not often enough. Recognize that if you have one concept (too much or too little), your partner probably holds the opposite view. Learn to structure your timing needs in order to benefit both of you. Use facilitative communicative skills to understand each other's personal timing better, and it is less likely that you will feel hurt or abused.

9. *Don't use coitus as a lever.* If your sex life is great, you probably aren't guilty of using sex as a retaliatory measure. Still, it bears mentioning that any time you participate—or refuse to participate—in coitus as a means to get your way, you create an interactional situation that becomes difficult to discuss in a positive manner. Don't do it!

10. *Be willing to do special things for your lover.* Both you and your partner may have certain preferences that don't equally excite the other. Recognize that in other areas of your relationship you willingly go places or do things that aren't quite as interesting or stimulating to the other. Be willing to show the same considerations in the coital relationship. That goes for both of you. There is a certain delight in having someone you care about show special concern. Be considerate and giving to your partner in coital aspects in much the same way that you are caring in other areas of your relationship.

11. *Learn to listen.* Nothing is more frustrating than talking to someone who isn't concentrating on what you say. It shows. Yet few of us are good listeners. Perhaps that is why you appreciate a good listener, but it takes practice and work, because years are spent not listening—or at least not listening actively. Here are some reasons why you avoid listening. You concentrate on what you are going to say as soon as the other person finishes what he or she has to say. You disagree with what is being said, so you feel there is no point in listening. You are disinterested in the other person or in the subject matter. You concentrate on other matters, future or past. You experience emotional or physical discomforts.

Good listening is simply a matter of getting rid of bad habits. You'll be surprised at how much more you begin to hear what is said once you learn to listen actively. And other people appreciate a good listener. Don't you?

HOW TO DEAL WITH COITAL PROBLEMS

Even the best relationships hit snags. But when you know how to communicate through difficult times, problems can change to increased growth and awareness about the relationship. Remember that when couples don't learn to talk through trying times without leaving a residue of bitterness, there may not be many more good times.

When problems relate to coital concerns, the talking-out process can feel like a "walking on eggs" situation. Nevertheless, it is important to discuss many of the concerns that won't fade with time. Left untended, your annoyances or hurt feelings can fester like an infection until the relationship must be terminated.

When coital problems need to be discussed between partners, remember these guidelines for building constructive talks:

1. *Use positives.* The old adage, "You catch more flies with honey than with vinegar," certainly applies to good coital communication. Most people respond better to positives than to negatives. You tend to listen more carefully when someone addresses you with positive messages. Conversely, you tend to leap to your own defense when given negative messages. For example, instead of saying "I don't like it when you . . ." try "When you do . . . I feel really good." Remember that you may not be comfortable speaking in positives. It may take a bit of practice for it to feel right.
2. *Keep in the present.* Don't be tempted to bring up past

events or conversations, and especially don't parade past failures. This is generally done as a retaliatory tactic to hurt the other partner below the belt: Rarely is the past brought up in order to contribute facilitative elements to the conversation.
3. *Avoid always or never statements.* Don't allow yourself to say "You always . . ." or "You never. . . ." Remember that you are concerned about creating better understanding about this one situation. Bringing in the whole world of hurt feelings guarantees that the disagreement becomes too great to resolve.
4. *Be succinct.* Don't go on for paragraphs describing in minute details every nuance of your feelings. Make your point simply and directly.
5. *A matter of timing.* Select the time for discussion carefully. Times when your partner is getting ready for work or when it is late at night will scarcely bring about the receptive communication that you desire. Also, be aware that during the discussion one of you may become too upset to continue the talk. When this happens, you invite World War III unless both agree to resume at a later time. It may only require a thirty-minute interval, or perhaps a longer time is needed. Settle on the schedule mutually, and keep your word. Also, agree on a time limit for the talk.
6. *Avoid rightness–wrongness discussions.* When you declare yourself right, you allow the unspoken or spoken message to imply that your partner is wrong. Don't discuss coital situations in a win–lose fashion—when one person is right, the other is automatically wrong. One-upmanship will not bring about greater understanding—only greater misunderstanding. It becomes a balance sheet scorecard for the purpose of being right more often than wrong.

    Make a choice. Do you want to be right, or do you want to build a more meaningful relationship? It makes a difference in how you argue. If your goal is always to be right, then your goal can't also seek for better understanding in the relationship. Think about it. Which is more beneficial to you?

FACILITATIVE SEXUALITY EQUALS RESPONSIBLE SEXUALITY

Responsible sexuality is more than deciding when or with whom you are going to have coitus. It is much more than that. Responsible sexuality involves having the necessary communication skills to bring about a mutual, sharing, and facilitative coital experience. It means learning to be more comfortable about yourself and with your partner. It means deciding to be positive and facilitative and being able to cast out harmful fears about being hurt or betrayed.

When you work to develop positive communication, the opportunities increase for feeling happy with your sexual self and for enjoying coital experiences to the fullest. You build a facilitative relationship. As you read the following five important considerations, remember that you won't be very facilitative in bed if you aren't facilitative out of bed.

1. *Encourage freedom.* Allow both individuals the right to be exactly that—individuals. That is, allow room for freedom. Freedom does not mean a lack of morality, nor is it a carte blanche for sex with others. Freedom also does not suggest a lack of concern. Rather, freedom is letting go of the fears, anxieties, and games that you play because you are afraid. Freedom is encouraging the other person to grow fully in ways that are positive. That often means that one person becomes less dependent on the other. It often involves allowing one person the right to assume a hobby or job that gives less time to you—and vice versa. In essence, freedom is giving and having permission to be who you are.

2. *Stop experiencing yourself through stereotypes.* As long as

you cling to the rubber stamp of what males or females are supposed to be, you reduce positive acceptance of yourself and others. Stereotypes cry out for conformity. To be exactly like everyone else—a carbon copy.

Sexual stereotypes demand that you must walk, talk, dress, act, and think in specified manners. When you live in stereotypes, you reduce the potential to relax and maximize sexual pleasure. You are, instead, too concerned about sexually acting and reacting in terms of perceived appropriate stereotypes. As a result of these restrictions, you accept no less from members of the opposite sex. Moreover, you may pass up some super males or females because they don't fit or live those stereotypes. The most worthwhile work that you can pursue in life is to dare to be yourself. And it is work! So stop being a composite of everybody else in the world. Be yourself. Celebrate life. Why spend this one short lifetime being a collection of other people?

3. *Don't box others into stereotypes.* Once you begin to experience the delight and freedom of simply being yourself, the next step is to allow others the same right to go beyond stereotypic boundaries. Don't restrict or hurt your partner through unjust stereotypic expectations, such as belief that males should be strong, aggressive, and independent or that females must be passive, weak, and dependent. Don't accept the harmful stereotypes of double standard thinking that create different rules for males and females. Develop, instead, an equal standard for both. Let your partner enjoy the right to be more than a socially approved image.

4. *Seek changes; take risks; expect improvements.* The good life is a series of accepted changes and personal growth. You must be willing to change and grow and to admit the need for change and growth. Neither you nor your partner will be exactly the same tomorrow or next year. Few couples live together for twenty years with the same

set of mutual dreams and goals. Yet seldom do couples sit down and talk about their changing dreams and goals as they once did in the beginning. People change; dreams change; goals change; and needs change. It is therefore crucial to the positive continuance of a relationship for you both to talk about—and deal with—changes in personal needs and goals.

Although change can be frightening, it can lead to growth, maturity, and personal strength. You wouldn't want to be at thirty, for example, the same person you were at twenty. Life is a series of stages of growth and change, or it is a sameness of stagnation. For example, when marriage is a strong commitment, wedding vows are just the beginning phase of the work; the readjustments and the changes bring about the best for the individuals as well as for the couple. When a person says, "Well, I simply am the way I am, I can't change," he or she is often telling something about his or her inflexibility. A good relationship is a series of necessary changes and readjustments. Taking on the risk of change when necessary brings about happiness and success.

5. *Create new language habits.* You are what you think you are. Responsible sexuality means being yourself to the best of your ability—no excuses, no blaming, and no language handicaps. Become conscious that language strengthens attitudes and therefore influences your sexual and coital behaviors. If those language habits are formed in put-downs about yourself or others, set about to change those negative ways of interacting. Your language is you. Change the language, and you can positively change your sexuality. Get rid of excuses, blaming, and language handicaps, such as messages of "I should" and "my duty."

What do you gain from facilitative and responsible sexuality? You and your partner both benefit as a result of efforts to develop these skills. The male can stop being expected to perform. He can stop trying to prove himself. He can stop hiding fears about his emotions and instead be honest about his feelings. He doesn't have to be a sexual athlete. He doesn't have to pretend to possess a myriad of experiences and coital novelties. He hasn't failed when he can't get an erection, nor has he failed when his partner doesn't have an orgasm. And he isn't responsible for the success or failure of coitus.

The woman can identify her sexual needs and urges as being equally important to his. She can be the initiator when she wants to be. It means that she no longer sees herself as the passive partner. She touches, explores, and takes an equal responsibility for the pleasure each receives. She doesn't expect him always to be erect or always to have a climax. It means that she learns to help bring about an orgasm for herself by certain movements or positions. (Experiment! It's fun.) And she is not automatically to blame when they experience some kind of coital problem.

Finally, facilitative communication means that you as an individual—and you as a couple—learn to share your body and personality in such a way as to please yourself and your partner mutually.

To improve your sexpressions is to maximize your sexual pleasure. Overcome the negatives and polish up the positives. Begin . . . I wish you the best!

INDEX

A

Adolescence, peer communication in, 132–39
Adulthood, peer communication in, 139–44
Advertising, 155–61
Age, 53–54
Anti-male crusader, 142–43
Assumptions, 214–15
Avoidance, 115–16

B

Birth control, 174
Broverman, Inge, 183

C

Camaraderie, masculine, 81–82
Change, risk of, 222–23
Chastity, 102
Childhood discussions, 131–32
Clitoral orgasm, 32
Clitoridectomy, 103
Communication, 5–14
    double standard, 17, 43–45, 48–49, 57, 96–101
    learning facilitative, 212–24
    romantic, 104–6
    (see also Language; Peer communication; Sex education; Sexual gamesmanship)
Communication gap, 120–21
Comparisons, 17
Compliments, 217
Conformity, 132–39
Consciousness groups, 185
Cosmopolitan, 152
Council of Macon, 99
"Couples Syndrome," 58

D

Dependency, 82–83
Divorce, 52, 58
Double standard, 17, 43–45, 48–49, 57, 96–101
Duty, 201–3

E

Equality, sexual, 20, 22, 23, 50–51
Experts, sexual, 169–86
    finding competent, 184–86
    physicians, 176–81
    stereotypes, 181–84
    training, 172–76
Extramarital affairs, 23–24

F

Faking, 215–16
Fantasies, 6, 153, 216–17
Femininity, 20–21, 64–88
    double standard roles, 17, 43–45, 48–49, 57, 96–101
    gamesmanship and, 23–29, 32–39
    myths of, 66–76
    rituals of, 76–85
    role equalizations, 51
    role reversals, 50
    sexual revolution, 57–58
    (see also Sexual heritage)
Freedom, 221
Frustration, 6, 11

G

Gamesmanship, 10, 16–39
    changing, 37–39

current difficulties with, 18–21
current images, 32–33
"He swept me off my feet,"
  34–35
"I can't control myself," 34
"I'm a nice girl," 33–34
little boys games, 28
little girls games, 28–29
ostrich game, 35–36
quantity and quality of sexual
  talk, 30–31
reasons for, 21–28
sexual revolution game, 31–32
stud man image, 35
symptoms of, 36–37
Good-bad woman dichotomy,
  101–4
Good ole boy, 140–41
Guilt, 21

H

Hebrews, 98, 99
Hefner, Hugh, 46
"He swept me off my feet" game,
  34–35
Honesty, 6–7, 22, 123–24, 215

I

"I can't control myself" game, 34
Ignorance, 7, 8
"I'm a nice girl" game, 33–34
Immaculate Conception, Doctrine
  of the, 105
Impotency, 97
Independence, 83–85
Infatuation, 106
Inferiority, 77, 97, 98, 102
Innocence, images of, 20

J

Johnson, Virginia, 172
Jokes, 30
Jovan, Incorporated, 159–60

K

Kayser-Roth Intimate Apparel
  Company, Incorporated, 160
Kinsey, Alfred, 45–47

L

Ladies Home Journal, 151
Language, 81–82, 118, 125, 129–
  45, 192–208, 223
  duty, 201–3
  polarities, 203–4
  quantity and quality, 30–31
  "shoulds," 197–201
  silence, 204–6
Listening, 218–19
Little boys games, 28
Little girls games, 28–29
Little Mary Sunshine, 141–42
Living together, 58

M

Magazines, 150–55
Marriage, commitment to, 57–58
Masculinity, 20–21, 64–88
  double standard roles, 17, 43–
    45, 48–49, 57, 96–101
  gamesmanship and, 22–23, 26–
    28, 32–39
  myths of, 66–76
  rituals of, 76–85
  role equalizations, 51

role reversals, 50
sexual revolution, 57-58
(*see also* Sexual heritage)
Masters, William, 172
Master-slave premise, 25
Masturbation, 114, 116-17
Mata Hari, 142
Media, 8, 10, 149-65
  magazine advertisements, 155-61
  magazines, 150-55
  sex manuals, 161-64
  sexual revolution and, 44, 45-47, 53
Medical students, 179-80
Modesty, 179
Myths, 7
  of masculinity and femininity, 66-76
  of sexual revolution, 51-56

N

New Woman, 154
"Normal" activities, 55-56

O

Oral sex, 170-71
Orgasm, 32, 97, 162-63, 202
Ostrich game, 35-36

P

Parents, 8, 10, 29 (*see also* Sex education)
Paternity, 99
Peer communication, 8, 10, 129-45
  adolescent, 132-39
  adulthood, 139-44
  childhood discussions, 131-32
  developing constructive, 144-45
Perfection, 106
Petting, 29
Physical appearance, 54, 77-78
Physicians, as sexual experts, 176-81
Playboy, 45-47, 153, 154
Playboy Image, 33, 141
Playgirl, 154
Polarities, 203-4
Promiscuity, 100
Property rights, 98
Pure Virgin, image of, 48, 101-4

R

Redbook, 154
Rejection, 78-81, 136, 196
Retaliation, 20, 218, 220
Rightness-wrongness discussions, 220
Rituals of masculinity and femininity, 76-85
Role equalizations, 51
Role reversals, 50
Romantic communication, 104-6

S

Same-sex communication, 9-10, 129-45
Seductress Eve, image of, 48, 101-4
Self-worth, 65-66
Sensitivity, 14, 215
Sex education, 111-25
  avoidance, 115-16

communication gap, 120-21
lecture versus discussion, 116-17, 124-25
materials for, 122-23
reasons for parents' failure in, 117-20
(*see also* Peer communication)
Sex manuals, 161-64
Sexpressions, defined, 11
"Sex Role Stereotypes: A Current Appraisal" (Broverman), 183
Sexual Behavior of the Human Female (Kinsey), 45-47
Sexual drive, 102, 176
Sexual gamesmanship (*see* Gamesmanship)
Sexual heritage, 8, 19, 94-107
   double standard, 17, 43-45, 57, 96-101
   romantic communication, 104-6
   seductress Eve/Virgin Mary images, 48, 101-4
Sexual language (*see* Language)
Sexual liberation, 18, 20
Sexual revolution, 43-59
   defined, 49-51
   double standard, 43-45, 48-49, 57
   media and, 44, 45-47, 53
   myths of, 51-56
   past traditions, 47-48
Sexual revolution game, 31-32
Sexual talk (*see* Language)
"Shoulds," 197-201
Silence, 204-6
Singleness, 52
Statistics, 55
Stereotypes, 10, 20, 64-66, 162-64, 181-84, 221-22

Strong and silent man's man, 140
Stud man image, 35
Subaru of America, 157-58
Superiority, 77, 97, 98, 137-38
Susie Sorority, 142

T

Tertullian, 102
Thoreau, Henry David, 135
Timid Tom, 141
Timing needs, 217-18
Tomboy behavior, 78
Total Woman Image, 33

U

Uncertainty, 11

V

Vaginal orgasm, 32
Virgin Mary, image of, 48, 101-4

W

Widowed people, 52

Y

Youth-oriented society, 53

Z

Zube, Margaret, 151